Full Experience Publishing

Full images and additional information on
www.fullexperienceliving.com

Copyright © Barry Bassett 2020
Cover Design © Josh Bassett 2020
Illustrations © Josh Bassett 2020

Barry Bassett has asserted his right under the Copyright, Designs and Patents Act, 1988 to be identified as the author of this work.

This book is sold subject to the condition that it shall not, by way of trade or otherwise, be lent, resold, hired-out, or otherwise circulated without the publishers prior consent, in any form of binding or cover, other than in which it is published and without a similar condition, including this condition, being imposed on the subsequent purchaser.

Typeset in Arial 11/15 point
Printed and bound by Amazon.

Jeffrey Syed Bassett

1941-2008

I dedicate this story to my Dad, who was a true innovator and entrepreneur.

Dad and I both made a lot of mistakes and whilst my journey from arrogant teenager to insightful adult, including an extraordinary recovery from near-certain bankruptcy, has been incredibly tough, were I to have my time all over again and without the benefit of hindsight, then I feel some comfort that I would live my life the same way without changing anything.

Sincere thanks to my extraordinarily talented son, Josh, for his amazing cover design and illustrations throughout this book.

"It is not the critic who counts; not the man who points out how the strong man stumbles, nor where the doer of deeds could have done them better.

The credit belongs to the man who is actually in the arena, whose face is marred by dust and sweat and blood; who at the worst, should he fail, at least fails while daring greatly, so that his place shall never be with those cold and timid souls who neither know victory nor defeat.

You have never lived, until you've nearly died and for those who have to fight for it, life truly holds a flavour the protected shall never know."

Theodore Roosevelt

Chapter 1.   Board Meeting
Board Meeting. VMI, London Monday 4 June 2007.

"What is the actual financial position as
of today?" I asked.

> "Well, we owe our suppliers £339K,
> VAT of £79K, £29K of PAYE and we
> also owe the Factoring company
> £120K", said Monika Bassett, my Mum.

"So, we actually owe almost £600K?

Wow." I said glumly.

"How much is in the bank?"

> "Actually, we have literally no money."

"Can it be any worse?" I asked.

> "Since the financial restructure of last
> year, we have not been able to keep up
> with the lease repayments either and
> are now £15,000 in arrears, so we are
> now in danger of having our cameras
> repossessed."

"It gets worse!"

…and the insurance company
DEFINITELY said that they wouldn't
honour the insurance claim from the

burglary? We were relying on that
£600K."

        "No. They told me definitively today
        that this was their final decision."

"BASTARDS! They could have told us
this six months ago so that we could
have cut our costs further instead of
waiting for a pay-out that they had no
intention of honouring.

And now it is just too late…," I said.

"We owe almost £600K which works out
at about five months of revenue; we
have very little equipment that wasn't
stolen which we can rent out and
actually earn us revenue; we owe £15K
in overdue leases and you are telling me
that we have NO MONEY?"

        "…and don't forget the £250K of
        personal guarantees that we have to
        the leasing companies if we go bust,"
        said Jeff Bassett, my Dad.

The three members of the board of VMI all looked at each other
grimly. Business failure looked certain.

"Right then, I am going to have to think
of a plan." I said.

This was met by silence.

"I'm off for a bike ride. Geneva to
Cannes through the Alps should do it.

1000km and 21 Alps. See you in two
weeks and I WILL have a plan."

Jeff Bassett, Barry Bassett & Monika Bassett (1990)

PART I

Chapter 2.   Early Years

Judgement comes from experience, and experience comes from bad judgement. Simon Bolivar

Learn from the mistakes of others. You can't live long enough to make them all yourself. Eleanor Roosevelt

My Dad taught me that if you see everyone running in one direction, then look at where they are coming from and consider running in that direction, as they may have all missed something.

The essence of this idea has come to define the person that I have become and for me, this started forming at a very early age.

Raised in North West London in 1968 from an immigrant family, it was never easy for me to fit in.

My Mum was the youngest of four sisters and born in Nuremberg in Northern Germany just after the war. Moving to London in her teens to work as an au pair, she had enrolled in a local college to improve her English and it was there that she met my Dad. Although she always meant well, her extremely matter of fact and blunt manner proclaimed that the world should take her as she was and this could come across as a bit abrasive.

Dad was the polar opposite. Born in Hyderabad in India, of Persian and Turkish parents, he was just five years old in 1947 when Pakistan was partitioned from India. Being Muslim, his entire family had to walk 1000 miles to Pakistan taking with them only what they could carry. I still can't imagine what that was like - he always told me that he still remembered two lines of people walking in opposite directions separated by a few metres during partition. He loved England and we all considered him to be more English than real Brits were!

Dad immigrated to the UK in his early twenties with a strong American accent which he had developed from watching American films and worked really hard to blend-in when he arrived in London. Instead of joining a Pakistani diaspora, he preferred to adopt local customs and over time, his accent became so polished, that you would never have known that he wasn't English. He was just a thoroughly nice guy and endeavoured to always be a perfect Gentlemen. Everyone who met him, loved him.

My parents had a pronounced laissez faire approach to parenting but the deep cultural differences between their Pakistani and Germanic backgrounds made for some interesting conflicts that would mould both me and my sister.

I think that Dad was embarrassed to be a Pakistani – remember that he arrived in the mid-1960s and there was a lot of racism in England. Consequently, he was always trying to be British and not stand out. When he and Mum first met, Dad was initially embarrassed to say that he couldn't eat pork for religious reasons and instead, told Mum that he didn't 'like' pork. Mum couldn't understand how this was even possible, since as a German, she had been brought up eating vast quantities of pork (and Germans cook pork extremely well). The story goes that she prepared him a delicious meal which they both really enjoyed and then after they had finished eating, she asked him what he had thought of the food and of course, he complemented her on her cooking. Dad recalls that her face broke into a big smile when she said, "…and you thought that you didn't like pork!"

It was obvious from the start that I would never fit in since everything that I saw of the world would be seen through the spectacles of both German and Pakistani values in 1970s Britain.

This was brought into sharp context some years later when I was 17 and an Uncle and Aunt came to stay for an extended period. My Aunt suffered a number of miscarriages in Karachi and had come to the UK with its better healthcare in order to complete her pregnancy. They stayed for several months and every day when Mum and Dad were at work, Auntie would cook wonderful curries and although her food was truly fantastic, I did eventually become fed-up of spicy food and learnt to cook for myself.

Every evening, Mum would serve the meal which Auntie had cooked and everyone would sit down to eat. After we had all finished, Mum would ask whether anyone would like any more and then, sensibly clear up when there were no takers for seconds.

Something very subtle was going on here but I would only find out several years later, that my Uncle was actually hungry after every meal but couldn't bring himself to ask for seconds and it turns out that he was visiting a curry house every lunchtime to buy boiled rice to eat before dinner. His reasoning? He was too embarrassed to ask Mum for seconds and desperately didn't want to make a fuss!

This is the exchange that he was expecting.

Pakistani version of asking for seconds at dinner (so as not to cause any offense)

"Would you like some more?"

"No thanks"
"Really? Please have some more."

"No really, I am full"
"I must insist – please have some more."

"OK, if you insist".

German version of asking for seconds at dinner

"Would you like some more?"

10

"Yes please."

So, you can see why the world must have been a confusing place for me!

While Dad had a very hands-off approach when I was growing up, education was extremely important to him. His Grandparents were apparently so wealthy that they had lived like kings and his Grandmother never wore the same outfit twice, donating all of her clothes to charity after wearing them. They then lost all of their money quite suddenly and from being really rich, they found that they now didn't have enough money to live.

My Great Grandad insisted that they would rather skip meals to buy books if this ensured that their sons could have the best education. From that troubled start, all five sons rose to the top of their professions and valuing education became strongly embedded in my Pakistani roots.

Mum was born into a working-class German family and her Dad had been a tailor and veteran of the Second World War. He may have been a skilled tailor but sadly, he was not a successful businessman so there was never very much money at home. Her Mum however, was a thrifty German housewife who managed to bring up four daughters alone during the war, which would have been extremely challenging and was testament to her resourcefulness. Likewise with Mum, existence and survival would define her values too.

Mum left school at 14 to go to secretarial college whereas Dad had been university educated. Valuing our education was very much my Dad's influence, but Mum was happy to support him.

Schools in North West London in the 1970s were poor and though my parents struggled financially, they managed to put my sister and I through prep school. They could not afford private secondary education, so Mum was determined to find the best state-run schools, since they felt that this would give us the greatest opportunity to go to university.

Mum is creative and enterprising and managed to persuade the local council to send me to a school outside our borough which had only recently changed from being a grammar school to a comprehensive. Whereas all grammar schools had very high standards and good teaching, they had no idea that by the time of its second comprehensive intake, the Westminster City School in Victoria, had gone rapidly downhill. It was also an hour's commute for me requiring a bus and two tube trains each way and made it doubly difficult for me to make friends. My parent's intentions may have been excellent but it wasn't a good decision.

The long commute put me off volunteering to take part in school plays and sports teams and as a result, I didn't have much of a social life and just a few close friends at school.

There was a lot of racism in 1970s Britain and being beaten up for being from an Asian background was fairly normal then. It even had a special word and a song – "Ding, dong the lights are flashing, we're going Paki bashing". It still makes me shudder today. I remember that leaving school and avoiding the skinheads was a challenge in itself, since beating up kids like me was fair sport to them.

Adolescence is a lonely time for boys and so it was for me. I wasn't one of the popular kids and didn't fit in wherever I went. After a while I realised that if I couldn't be like the others, then I should celebrate this and made a point of trying to be different. However, as I was to learn, this didn't really help me to make friends or lead to an easier life.

During this time, Dad was working from home in his workshop and I seemed to be very incidental to him. He would spend most of his time there and only come in for short bursts. Whenever he would see me, his face would break into a smile and he would say to me,

"Yes please!" This meant that I now had to make him a cup of coffee – milk and two sugars and he drank a LOT of coffee. We were early adopters of the Braun coffee machines and used them so much that they only lasted six months before needing replacing.

His attitude to me completely changed when it was time for either the termly school report or parents' evening, at which point he would become super-attentive and this would be followed by the inevitable family conference to work out why I hadn't performed well enough. For Dad, whilst A-grades were expected, these were sadly quite rare on my report cards and I grew up feeling that I always HAD to work harder and perform better if I wanted to win his approval. This seemed really unfair to me since he'd never been a great student himself. Nonetheless, sons of Pakistani fathers had to be respectful and I would never be so insolent as to make this point to him directly.

Dad once told me that, when he was a young father, he had asked a mother what she thought the secret of good parenthood was, and she had replied that it was important to let her children develop by allowing them to question her. It is a credit to him that he did allow me to question him and this gave me great self-confidence and independence, though it would also cause us significant problems later on.

I made an important decision when I was 13 that I would fully commit to being the A-grade student that Dad wanted me to be, in order to win his approval. I confess that I am not a natural student but have a great work ethic and studied as hard as I could and did really well that year. After the exam results were out, I was so proud with how well I had done. I ran home and told him that I had managed to achieve the second-highest score in the school in chemistry. I remember that he smiled wanly and replied, "Next time, be first!" That was it. No congratulations or a hug – just do better next time. These words still smart today.

Not going to a local school meant that I didn't have many local friends, so I decided to change this by joining the Air Cadets. Dad hated the army and initially didn't want to let me go, so I had to firmly argue my case in a family conference before he granted me his permission to join.

I really enjoyed Air Cadets and even learned to fly an aeroplane, though frustratingly for me, my attitude of trying to make myself act like an outsider had prevailed and found that I was never to be popular in this group either. The Commanding Officer also didn't like me, so while I passed all of the exams, I was never promoted beyond cadet.

It would take until my university years to fully discover the person that I was to become and how to turn my weaknesses into my strengths.

Barry skiing in 1983

§

Chapter 3.   Goatanomics

The optimist proclaims that we live in the best of all possible worlds; and the pessimist fears this is true.   James Branch Cabell, The Silver Stallion, 1926

Or the story of the man, his Mullah and a goat.

I read what I assume is an apocryphal story some years ago and I feel that the underlying message is so important, that I wanted to dedicate an entire chapter to it. A man visits his Mullah and laments that he is unhappy.

"My wife is unhappy, my children are crying and
  I don't have enough money. What do I
do?"

                                    "Buy a goat!"
"What!"

                                    "Buy a goat."
"…but…"

                                    "Buy a goat." (forcefully)

…and the man leaves the Mullah looking dejected.

He returns the next morning looking even more unhappy.

"My wife is unhappy, my children are
crying, I don't have enough money and

that BLOODY goat is shitting
everywhere! What do I do?"

                              "Sell the goat!"
"What!"

                              "Sell the goat."

"…but you told me to buy a goat."

                              "Sell the goat." (forcefully)

…and the man once again leaves the Mullah, though this time
looking even more dejected.

However, he returns the following morning but now looks a
completely changed man and this time, he is actually smiling.

   "I am SO HAPPY now that goat is gone!"

As I said earlier, I don't really think that the man, his Mullah or the
goat really existed but I often think that this story can teach us a
really important key to happiness. My thought process goes like
this.

We all live in our own bubbles and sometimes find ourselves entirely
consumed by problems which we know are not really that important
(pressing deadline; impossible target, too much to do; can't afford a
skiing holiday…) but these problems still manage to consume much
of our thinking time and this influences how we feel and live. We
stop enjoying our food, our families and may even start avoiding our
friends. We may appear pensive, distant and stressed and although
there may be so much that is good in our lives, at this specific
moment, we can't appreciate it.

All of those missed opportunities to have great experiences - what a
tragedy!

Then, when something really serious happens (terminal diagnosis; immanent financial ruin, a shark suddenly appears who is about to eat you, etc.) all of your previous problems instantly evaporate in a puff of smoke, as you now totally concentrate all of your attention to solving this serious, new problem.

I love to deliberate on the joy which we would suddenly experience were this new problem suddenly to disappear (you were given the wrong diagnosis; the bill was in Zimbabwean dollars; the shark was a vegetarian, etc.)

The problem is that we often can't appreciate the perspective and importance of these problems in the wider context of our everyday lives. When my wife presents me with a problem that she deems both serious and insoluble, she is never comforted when I tell her that at least she hasn't just stood on a landmine (since that would be much worse, or something equally banal).

"That's NOT very helpful," she always replies to me.

However, I think this approach can really be helpful to develop a sense of perspective for our problems and it reminds me to regularly reappraise how great life is here on planet Earth.

I don't think that we are particularly good at considering what is genuinely important to us.

I love the scene in Douglas Adams' *The Hitchhiker's Guide to the Galaxy*, when an extraordinarily arrogant character called Zaphod Beeblebrox is made to go into a terrifying machine called the Total Perspective Vortex, in order for him to see just how insignificant he is in the grand scheme of the universe. This machine is supposed to totally blow your mind when you see the vastness of the universe and just how puny and inconsequential we are in relation to it. The joke is that in the story, Zaphod becomes the first person to leave the Total Perspective Vortex chamber without going mad, since he now really believes that he is worthy of his important position in the galaxy. Being Galactic President in the story may have helped him to believe this!

When you consider that we live on one of eight planets in our solar system which orbit the sun in a galaxy called the Milky Way which itself comprises of an estimated 100 billion stars, and that this is just one of an estimated 100 billion galaxies, you realise how totally insignificant our planet and life on it becomes...

When I started studying for my MBA some years later, Barclays Bank was kind enough to offer me a £10,000 interest-free loan for my tuition fees (£10K doesn't go very far these days but in 1993, this was a fair sum of money).

Dad had volunteered for the company to pay for my MBA but I felt that an interest-free £10K was an offer too good to pass on, so I applied and soon had an additional £10,000 in my bank account and decided to buy a Supercar.

Although I couldn't really afford it, this new windfall enabled me to buy a two-year old Toyota Supra Turbo, which could travel 150mph, had leather upholstery, climate control, electric seats, air con and lights which flipped up and down (this was the early 1990s, remember). Most importantly, it was powered by a 3-litre turbocharged engine and if I double-declutched, put the car into second gear and floored it, then even at 70mph, I could squeal the tyres. For a 23-year old, this was heaven! However, where does this fit in with Goatanomics, I hear you ask?

Well, when the car was delivered, I was initially deliriously happy. But then I discovered a small problem with the transmission and I noticed that when I changed from first to second gear at less than 1600 revs, I could detect a faint noise coming from the engine that shouldn't have been there. It may have been a barely-audible whooshing/rattling noise but the important thing was that I could hear it and when I drove the car, this is what I listened out for. It drove me nuts!

Whilst my friends were really awed by how amazing this car was, all I could hear was this awful noise and I would make a point of drawing their attention to it every time!

Eventually I took it back to the dealer and they stripped and rebuilt the entire transmission, after which the noise disappeared - but for two weeks, I didn't enjoy my amazing new car. What a shame! - isn't this just like life?

You might be interested to know that we did take this car to the Alps (I called her Georgina) and drove extremely fast on the Autobahns, one time managing to hit 146mph (rain stopped me pushing on to 150mph. It's worth pointing out that there were no speed limits in place). When we returned from the trip, just two months after buying the car, I sold it, with my supercar craving having been satiated.

It is as true today as it was then, but a young man can't afford both a house and an extravagant car at the same time. Sometimes hard choices need to be made – I bought a house, so the car had to go.

I conclude from this lesson that if you can, take time out of every day to smell the flowers; look at the beautiful buildings and trees; take a walk; enjoy your coffee; spend quality time with your friends and family; slow down and consider whether your problems are really so serious that you can't enjoy the now.

In the words of Jack Nicholson's character Melvin in the film *As Good As It Gets,* the best things about life are described as 'good times and noodle salad'. If you haven't watched this film before, then it is a life changer and Melvin really did master the lessons of Goatanomics, although he didn't realise this at the time!

FULL EXPERIENCE LIVING

§

Chapter 4.   Challenge everything: Videomania

Human beings, who are almost unique in having the ability to learn from the experience of others, are also remarkable for their apparent disinclination to do so. Douglas Adams, "Last Chance to See"

I never met my Dad's Dad because he died before I was born but Dad always used to tell me that I was just like him. Apparently, my Grandad was a great sportsman and loved football; he had gymnastic rings installed in his garden and was a formidable competitor in every aspect of his life. The comparison ends here, since he also smoked 60 cigarettes a day, became a workaholic and died young and I have no intentions of following him here.

Dad would always tell me that you achieve what you aim for, so whilst work has always been very important to me, I have tried hard to not let my work totally dominate my life.

"The way to hell is paved with good intentions," is maybe an overused cliché but I'm reminded that the recovery from our uninsured loss in 2007 would cast a deep shadow in the years that followed for me and my family. The next 10 years became entirely work-orientated and much of this time was absolutely not fun. I must confess that I have definitely not always achieved a perfect work/life balance, though I've never stopped trying.

I was sadly never to meet Grandad but I knew he was a very senior figure at the Pakistan International Bank and at considerable personal financial cost, sent Dad to study Aeronautical Engineering in the UK in the mid-1960s.

Dad was a born engineer and if you ever had an engineering problem, then he would be the first person that you would turn to. His mind really didn't think like anyone else's. His solution might not be obvious or conventional but he wouldn't stop thinking about it until he had worked-out a solution.

He hated two things, which would come to mould his life.

1. Not being able to find a solution.
2. Being told that he couldn't do something.

He once had an idea that the way to solve the shortage of the world's resources was to genetically shrink everyone to half of their size. "If we did this, then we could have houses which were half of the size that they are now and create twice as many resources," he claimed… Amazingly, I found out recently that this same idea was taken to be the plot in a 2017 Matt Damon film called *Downsizing*.

When I was about eight, Dad and I embarked on a project to create the world's first Perpetual Motion Machine and our ambitious aim was to harness a previously unused form of energy, which we called Magnetic Energy. We called this top-secret experiment, Project X.

…and we even created the First Law of Perpetual Motion:

> **Perpetual Motion is only possible in a crossed magnetic field.**

We bought a lot of strong, expensive, industrial magnets and created our early prototypes which were designed to rotate forever without using any external energy. They were incredible and totally challenged conventional physics and thinking.

The success of this project was going to be mind-blowing and widespread adoption would solve all of the world's energy problems. We were confident that we could provide a solution to entirely avoid the need to burn fossil fuels and look forward to mankind's future of clean energy.

Obviously, it didn't work. Firstly, we are not multi-billionaires and secondly, because there isn't such a thing as Magnetic Energy.   Some years later whilst studying physics at university and learning all about the conservation of energy laws, I realised that that we were totally barking up the wrong tree, although it clearly demonstrated that the process of independent thinking was alive in the both of us.

Just before he died, Dad was working on the concept of a fold-up bicycle that you would wear. (Yes, wear!) He never finished it and sadly I couldn't make sense from his notes, so it never saw reality.

Shortly after arriving in the UK, he realised that he didn't want to study aeronautical engineering after all and instead switched to an electronic engineering course. It was at this time that he met my Mum.

She initially considered him a terrible show-off and didn't like him at all. Then one day, they were both to attend a college outing to Brighton and everyone was told to bring a packed lunch. My German Mum prepared sandwiches, drinks and snacks, all very organised in a proper picnic set, while Dad arrived with a loaf of uncut French bread, a packet of butter, a hunk of cheese and didn't even bring a knife!

It is a commonly held belief that opposites attract and whatever the merits of this idiom, Monika and Jeff became an item from that day onwards and a year later, I arrived. Dad had a job working on kidney machines at an industrial company. He was intelligent, hard-working and was quickly promoted through the ranks, becoming the youngest supervisor that the company had ever had.

However, he wasn't happy and dreamt of being his own boss, so at the end of one of his annual reviews, after being told that he would not be receiving a raise, he made an impulsive decision and left his job. "…but Mr Bassett, you are already the highest paid member of your team – please be reasonable!"…

But this just wasn't his way though.

With a mortgage, young family and no job, it clearly wasn't the ideal time for him to go to the bank and ask for a loan, but Dad wasn't one for convention and the exchange with his bank manager during the ensuing meeting, went a bit like this.

"Good morning, Mr Bank Manager. I'd like a loan please."

"No, no Mr Bassett, you have misunderstood why I have called you here -

I want to know when you are going to reduce your overdraft!"

"Well we can discuss that another time.

Actually, I would like a loan please, as I am about to start a business."

"OK, what is your business idea?"

"I am not really sure, as I haven't decided yet but I would like a loan of £500 in order to start this business…"

That is honestly what happened and I don't know exactly how he did it but by the end of the meeting, Dad had agreed a loan with the National Westminster Bank for £500 and his company, J.Bassett and Co was born.

He initially started his business by buying and selling used cars from home and he would visit the Dagenham car auction every week and return with two or three cars that he had bought. Then he would service them and repair the bodywork himself in his workshop, which was attached to the side of our house and then sell them on for a tidy profit.

I remember that he was quite successful at this and it motivated me to buy and sell cars when I first left university, though it was only ever a side line for me. I would buy cars privately or at an auction (though only ever one at a time) and keep them for a few months before selling them on for a small markup. I only ever did it as a bit of fun and for the first few years of my career, all of my motoring was effectively free, though bodywork and car mechanics remained strictly Dad's domain.

As a true entrepreneur with an eye to the future, my Dad began buying and selling used black and white and then later, colour televisions from home and like with cars, he would repair them in his workshop. During the mid-1970s when TVs were incredibly expensive, these magnificent and expensive Television Sets were more like pieces of furniture than items of consumer electronics, with large bulbous rear cabinets to protect a long protruding valve. In those days, a short while after you switched off the TV, a bright white dot would appear in the centre of the screen before it faded away.

I remember a French polisher would visit our home every week with his toolbox of special coloured brown paints, to repair the wooden TV cabinets that were ready to sell, and transform scratched wooden TV sets to look like new. For a while this business was really profitable, but like all good things, it too came to an end and he was soon on the lookout for a new opportunity.

Dad loved telling the story of what happened next, when a wealthy Irishman visited his workshop. Dad asked him to see something amazing. Apparently, they watched a few seconds of a cartoon which was on a TV at the time, after which Dad pressed a few buttons on an unfamiliar machine and then pressed a button which said 'play'. The customer was amazed and rendered speechless for a time, when exactly the same cartoon that he had just been watching, appeared once again on the TV. "I don't know what it is but I'll give you £100 for it!" Dad would say in a strong Irish accent repeating what the man had told him, before bursting into laughter!

It is truly hard to believe but until this time, you could only watch TV programmes at the time of transmission and after that, you had missed it. The invention of the video recorder would be transformative for all of us.

Dad began selling early video cassette recorders from his garage in the late 1970s. The Phillips N1500s that he sold were the very earliest video recorders and used the now obsolete 'VCR' format. The video cassettes were large and clunky as they were designed with two reels placed on top of each other (rather than the later VHS tapes, which had reels side by side).

At first, business in these novel machines was swift but these truly expensive video recorders were also very niche and did not endure. Business quickly tailed-off when Phillips introduced a long-play version a couple of years later. In fact, trade for Dad became so weak, that for the best part of a year, he earned virtually no income and we became genuinely poor.

He was a very proud man and although entitled to unemployment benefit, he refused to claim, telling us that he would prefer to die than join a dole queue (and I am not exaggerating). By now, my sister had been born and Mum, as a practical woman, made sure that she was working part time so that they had at least some income. I remember that these were really tough times and to make it doubly hard, they were now having to pay for two sets of school fees for my sister and I. However, this very skinny period saw my Dad working on a new idea with which he would win big.

Early Phillips VCR machines would only record for one hour onto a single video cassette, which meant that all feature films had to be recorded onto two separate tapes. He had an original idea to convert the early VCR machines to record long-play and this would avoid people needing to replace their recorders. Since the new long-play models were really expensive, he reckoned that he could charge people a lot of money to do this.

In order to achieve this, he would need to replace the video heads (the most expensive part of the recording/playback mechanism) and grind down the spindle which controlled the speed that the tape passed through the machine, extremely accurately. It is very hard to appreciate how hard a technical feat this was but it became very clear that this would not be easy when everyone that Dad explained this idea to, told him that he would need to work to an accuracy of several hundred thousandths of an inch and that it was *impossible* to do.

Dad loved nothing less than being told that something was impossible, so with their last savings, he returned from an auction one day carrying a pile of large dirty hunks of metal into his workshop, and didn't surface for three days.

He had bought a used lathe machine and stripped, degreased, sandblasted and rebuilt this magnificent device, then spraying it entirely orange. He then made a custom jig using Reynolds P38 car filler onto which he mounted a dentist drill at a critical angle, so that it could be moved in a very accurate and controlled way by the lathe machine. He fitted the drill with a grinding wheel embedded with industrial diamonds and finally, he was ready to build a prototype.

The prototype worked brilliantly, so he put an advert in the *Exchange and Mart*, which was the 1970s version of eBay as a weekly, printed magazine and very soon he had his first customer.

"This will either work, or they will return their video machine to me demanding a refund, and we will be ruined," he told us with a grim expression on his face.

It did work however and soon people were queuing up to have their video machines converted, and during this time, I also created a side line to earn additional pocket money for myself. Early VCR tapes cost around £30 each, which was a lot of money then and occasionally these tapes would snap when they finished rewinding, so I used to repair them for a fiver. This was a skilled process, since if the videotape wasn't accurately spliced or the splice was on the wrong side of the tape, then it could damage the customer's video machine. However, as a diligent 12-year old, I was very careful and used the money earned to fuel my new passion – computers.

As an aside here, the test tape that Dad used to test the long-play conversions was James Bond's, *Diamonds Are Forever*. This film, which I have come to love, was always playing in his workshop and I have watched it over eighty times and we always quote from it at home.

> "It's late, I'm tired, and there's still so much to do."
> Ernst Stavro Blofeld. Diamonds are Forever, 1971

In his spare time, Dad had a project to take apart the latest Phillips N1700 video machine and modify it to work from 12V. He had actually built the world's first portable video recorder based on the VCR format and Phillips were really interested in buying his prototype design but before they could do so, JVC had released the super-successful VHS format and overnight, this killed both Dad's business and the VCR format. It was time, once again, for a new idea.

My parents had two ideas for a new business – either personal computers or consumer video. Both were brand-new at the time but they knew nothing about computers and consumer video would build on what they already knew, so they rented a shop to sell the latest VHS video machines and colour TVs.

Videomania Ltd began trading from a retail shop premises close to where they lived in NW London at the start of January 1979. An inauspicious start meant that it very nearly didn't survive the first four months.

My parents fitted the best security that they were advised to and could afford, but the commercial door locks and internal roller shutters were no match for the determined burglars who wanted to steal the latest big thing. Within a week of opening, they had suffered their first break-in and the entire first stock was stolen by burglars using nothing more sophisticated than a crow bar, to jemmie open the front door.

The insurance company told them to fit an additional door lock, which they did and subsequently replaced their stock from savings, since it would be weeks before the insurance pay-out would be received.

However, just two days later, they were broken into in exactly the same way and once again, everything was stolen.

On the insurance company's instructions, a third door lock was fitted and they had to pay for yet another stock replacement. Surely they would be safe now?

Sadly not. This time, the persistent burglars ram-raided them by driving a vehicle through the shopfront and clearing them out yet again. When this happened, they still hadn't received any insurance money from even the first burglary, and had absolutely no money left to replace their stock and their future was uncertain.

They fitted large external roller shutters to replace the internal ones to stop ram-raiders in the future, and having the ear of a sympathetic bank, meant that they could finally afford to replace their stock once more and Videomania properly began selling consumer video machines to the public in the early 1980s.

Within four years however, increasing competition in a rapidly growing market, meant that margins had eroded and Monika and Jeff Bassett, who were now working together, were on the lookout once more for new opportunities.

A new market of professional video equipment was developing from the broadcast television industry and Dad was quick to notice that margins were higher selling professional products compared with the low margins selling domestic ones. They decided to change direction.

Gradually, the firm concentrated on selling used professional equipment and built up a loyal client base that purchased professional cameras and editing suites in order to shoot corporate and wedding video programmes, which at the time were brand new markets.

Dad maintained a workshop which was now based in the shop in Neasden, so that he could service and repair the professional machines, and for a while the level of business grew steadily. He wanted a new challenge and set up an edit suite in the upstairs of the premises and even built a small studio so that he could shoot and edit commercials and corporate programmes, while Mum concentrated on selling used professional TV gear downstairs. They expanded and even took on an additional employee called Ahmed, who was a lifelong friend, to run the service department.

This new formula worked fine for a few years, when Dad had another idea that they could hire out unsold cameras from their used equipment stock to clients and earn a fee twice over.

Whilst it was a brilliant concept, it wasn't a great business, due to poor standards and a lack of regular stock. The unreliable equipment and lack of quality control meant that it was unprofessionally run and soon developed a terrible reputation. Since the stock was always changing, advanced bookings were difficult because they couldn't rely on a specific camera still being available to hire by the time that the client wanted to hire it and, as a result, hire revenues remained low.

Very soon though, I would join the firm and change everything.

Videomania Shop in Neasden during 1980s

Chapter 5.   Computers

A pessimist sees the difficulty in every opportunity; an optimist sees the opportunity in every difficulty. Winston Churchill

From aged 13 onwards, I was always involved in the family business. In the early 1980s, when it was a consumer video store, the shop ran a video club and I would work on Saturdays checking-out and returning VHS films (*Attack of the Killer Tomatoes* was a popular spook horror film title!).

Although it seems strange now, I began filming events to earn extra money from that young age. Initially, clients who had bought their camera equipment from Mum and Dad would hire me when they were double-booked and I would film their bar mitzvahs, parties and later weddings for them too. In hindsight, it must have seemed really odd for a 13-year old to be filming a wedding but I just accepted it as normal and actually did a really great job, since I had started young and had had lots of practice. I even developed a technique of editing 'on the fly', so that when I filmed people dancing to music, I would carefully cut on the beat, so that the finished tape would look like it had been edited because there were rarely any jump-cuts in the music.

As soon as I turned 17, I bought a car from the savings I had earned and this made filming weddings much easier, since I could now film without needing someone else to do the driving. Also, being able to borrow equipment for free from the shop, made this a really good arrangement for me.

In fact, not only did I earn extra cash to help me through university but I would continue to film weddings at weekends into my early twenties and left university virtually debt-free.

I do recall one time during the summer holidays when I was 13 and working in the shop, Dad asked me to jump in the van, since we were going to film the 1982 International Country and Music Festival. Apparently, a camera operator had turned up drunk that morning and Dad was furious and had sent him home but this now left him short of a crew member and he thought that I could fill his place. I didn't question him and together we drove to a massive events tent in Peterborough and set-up our equipment for a two-camera live mix with one camera and the mixing equipment being installed on a gantry hanging 15m in the air and the second camera set up by the stage. We had brought the latest intercom system with us which you wore as a headset, and the system was designed to broadcast when it detected the sound of a voice. Obviously, Dad hadn't reckoned on one camera being placed so close to a massive bank of speakers which was enough volume to trigger the headset to permanently broadcast, and as a result, the system didn't work at all.

We improvised a technique to communicate remotely without intercom, where I would operate the vision mixer and was close enough to hear Dad's instructions. In order to communicate with the stage camera, he held one end of a long rope which we stretched across the framework under the tent roof and hung down to the camera operator, where we tied it to his collar. When Dad wanted to cut to the stage, he would tug on the rope and when the camera operator felt a tug on his collar, he would instantly stop moving the camera. It was remarkably primitive but did actually work.

Initially, Dad would call out, "To me! To James!", whereupon I would press the appropriate buttons on the mixer and perform the cuts or fades that he wanted. After about half an hour, he realised that he was no longer calling the shots, since the images on the main monitor were changing correctly by themselves. Would you believe, that for the entire three-day shoot, I mixed the cameras alone and even earned my name to be included on the end credits as *Vision Mixer.*

Computers had always been a major part of my life and I still remember the excitement as the early computers were developed and became cheap enough for me to afford. I immersed myself into mastering the technology, learning to write different computer programming languages and even discovering the joys of hacking (more on this, later...). I emerged from being a teenager with few friends to becoming a master of my universe because, as I was to discover, I had a very logical mind and was very good at computers.

When my parents were deciding whether they should make the transition for their business into either consumer video or computers at the end of the '70s, Mum brought home our first personal computer, called a Commodore PET and I was immediately hooked.

The idea was that my parents would learn all about computers and decide whether they would build a computer business or a video business and whilst Mum did attend a computer course, to put it kindly, she was not geek material. I, on the other hand had found my vocation…

I loved the challenge of learning about computers and from the luminous green screen, the integral cassette tape storage and the feeble 8K memory of the Commodore PET, I loved that computer. Much to the irritation of Dad though, this massively expensive machine spent most of its time playing Space Invaders which my friends and I became remarkably good at.

With the money that I'd earned from filming weddings and parties, I bought all the latest computers when they were released – firstly, the Sinclair ZX Spectrum, then the Commodore 64 and after that, the hard drives and additional peripherals. Finally, I also bought a modem, so I could for the first time, interface with external computers decades before the invention of the internet.

I mastered the BASIC computer language, followed by PASCAL, COBOL and FORTRAN. In my spare time, I wrote an application for a friend to build a relational database for his photography clients, which would allow him to do his invoicing and send reminders of which clients to call when their anniversaries were due.

I even wrote what we would now call a chat program, so that across a data network, two people could type and the cursor would work out where it needed to be on the page and curser up and across by the correct number of spaces to display the letters received before returning to add the letters which I would type to send. These early computers were much too slow to do this effectively using the built-in BASIC language program, so I explained the problem to my best friend, who was a computer prodigy. He said that I needed to learn machine language and this would speed things up. This meant that I would need to master Z80 and 6502 assembler code but he told me that it would be *much too hard for me to learn and that I would never master it…*

You can probably guess that this infuriated me, so I bought a book on Z80 assembler and wrote my application and it worked very well! Like Dad, I hate being told that I cannot do something!

Of course, my programming skills came in useful to take existing commercial games software and remove the security code which prevented them from being copied and then share them with my many geek-friends. This was the early Wild West of hacking and long before computer viruses had been even thought of.

Owning a modem opened up a completely new set of challenges for me. For the first time, I would be able to interface with other computers and could try to gain access to them. In those days, in order to connect to another system, you first had to make a telephone call, but before you did this, you had to find out the correct number to call and these were not widely publicised; then you needed to configure your modem to match that of the host network, which was another trial and error challenge and only then could you start to try to hack it. People in the early 1980s were not particularly judicious about choosing high security passwords, so we had great fun accessing many mainframes, which for a teenager was extremely exciting.

Studying now took second place to computers and, as you might expect, my schoolwork suffered.

My parents were doing better financially and could once again afford private education for me, so I changed schools to attend John Lyon School in Harrow for my sixth form. There I re-joined many of my peers from my early prep school again but it was very clear that we had all changed and I never really felt at home.

The teaching was better but it didn't help that five years of comprehensive education meant that I was now, way behind in maths and physics and utterly hated my third subject of economics. I had really wanted to study chemistry but Dad had steadfastly refused to allow it. He kept repeating that, "Economics would be good for business…" and at the time, I wasn't strong enough to stand up to him.

I did get my own back on the economics teacher, who would arrive on a Thursday morning for our double economics lesson looking really tired. This was because I had found out his home telephone number and programmed my computer to dial him up at random times during the night and then hang up when he answered. Not having a digital exchange had its benefits of course, as my call couldn't be tracked. Whilst I was never caught, I regret that I never apologised to him for my childish behaviour either.

After two years of A-Levels, I did just about well enough in my exams to win a university place at Keele University to study physics and maths and this was a perfect fit for me. By some strange paradox, being distracted by messing about with computers in my teens meant that studying computer engineering was no longer an option for me. I didn't mind though, as it meant that I was leaving home and would have my independence at last.

I had worked hard all summer and saved several hundreds of pounds filming weddings and I was ready for the next chapter in my life - university.

Chapter 6.   The science of great coffee and amazing eggs

A creative man is motivated by the desire to achieve, not by the desire to beat others. Ayn Rand

I consider the challenge of making better coffee and scrambled eggs to be a perfect microcosm of life and illustrates our different approaches to improving it, so ask you bear with me, as I explain the lengths which I went to, to achieve this.

For most of us, coffee is really important and by coffee, I mean, really good coffee.

The Italians have an honorary title for one who is able to master making a sublime Cappuccino as 'Barista' and whilst this name is now commonplace to describe the staff at the many coffee shops which adorn our high streets, this was not so when I started my search 30 years ago for the challenge of making the perfect cup of coffee and had to discover the secrets on my own.

I was always curious to learn any tips which might help me to improve my coffee-making skills and earn the right to call myself 'Barista'.

Cappuccino should be strong, rich but also creamy and light with delicately foamed milk and drinking it at home was never the same as a perfect barista-prepared coffee and I wanted to find out how to do this.

Of strange relevance to this too is that my family has also always enjoyed making scrambled eggs, which has been a traditional Saturday morning breakfast treat for us. Around 10 years ago I discovered that the science of preparing both scrambled eggs and making great cappuccino was related and it is all down to our underappreciated friend, the Lactobacillus Casei protein.

First, what makes a great coffee?

It wants to be delicately roasted, freshly ground, then prepared with the right strength and served at the perfect temperature. I first bought Italian Expresso machines (spend the extra for stainless steel, rather than aluminium, as they last ten times longer) and would heat these on my gas hob and they always made consistently good expresso coffee.

I sometimes noticed that prepared coffee could be horribly bitter and realised that some cafés did not clean out their machines properly prior to preparing coffee, and this caused the bitterness. Also, they would often squirt a fresh, hot expresso into a cold cup which would immediately cool my coffee, and who likes cold coffee?

My simple solution to solving both of these problems is to prepare an expresso shot into your cup, initially without using any coffee and then discard this water. This simultaneously heats and cleans the expresso filter of old coffee, and also warms your cup. If you don't own a conventional expresso machine (though you will probably want to after reading this chapter) then you can use hot water from a kettle instead to heat your cup.

After learning this simple lesson, I found that making good expresso wasn't hard but preparing the creamy milk became the challenge.

Wikipedia describes Microfoam as shiny, slightly thickened milk which should have microscopic, uniform bubbles. It is not as viscous or "foamy" as macrofoam – it is better described as "gooey" and resembles melted marshmallows or wet paint. There have been a variety of names used for this ideal standard, such as "microfoam", "velvet milk", "microbubbles", and so forth…

But how do you make it at home?

I started by heating the milk in a small jug to 65 degrees C. Instead of a microwave, I heated it on the hob and carefully monitored it using a milk thermometer, the way that baristas often do, and which I found gave me more control. I discovered that achieving the optimal temperature was crucial to avoid scalding the milk and destroying the coffee. Then I would create the foam by whizzing-up the heated milk using a battery-operated frother and the result wasn't bad. My frustration was that it just wasn't great.

Similarly when I prepared scrambled eggs, they had a perfect jelly-like consistency sometimes, but at other times they were not so good and I didn't understand why.

As I said at the start of this chapter, I consider the challenge of making better coffee and scrambled eggs to be a perfect microcosm of life and illustrates our different approaches to improving it.

I find that if you don't like something in your life, you have only three options.

1. Do nothing and accept it how it is. Perhaps great coffee and perfect eggs aren't that important to you.
2. Change something
3. Wait a bit and approach this problem at a later date. Wait a minute – this is the same as 1!

In practice, this means either being happy to leave things as they are and accept that they will not improve. Or to make a concerted decision to change something, which may improve things, though you would risk that it might actually make things worse.

Faced with this stark choice, I wasn't prepared to accept second class coffee and inconsistent eggs, so I bought new coffee machines, experimented heating milk to different temperatures and other strategies but I still wasn't totally happy with the results.

A twentieth anniversary reunion at Keele saw me attending a guest lecture on the science of food which really helped me to understand what was going on and from this point forward, both my coffee and scrambled eggs improved in quality and consistency and I wanted to share this lesson with you.

The L Casei protein (or Lactobacillus Casei in full) is present in fermented dairy products and is widely considered to have beneficial properties for human health.

This protein exists naturally in full-fat, semi-skimmed and also skimmed milk and is the active protein that gives both milk and eggs their specific properties when heated. For reference, the froth comes from the L Casei protein, not the fat and this explains why you can make milk foam with skimmed milk.

What is also really interesting is to understand what happens when it is heated. Unlike many foods which liquify when you heat them, L Casei chains first break apart and then tangle to make a jelly-type consistency and eventually knot-up, turning into a hard, dry solid - this is entirely consistent with what happens when you overcook eggs and they go dry.

So, if your goal is to make microfoam in order to enjoy a great cappuccino, then the only way to create small bubbles in your milk is to begin to agitate it and introduce just the right amount of air during the heating process. The key is to start the process when the milk is cold and then stop when the milk is at the right temperature and to achieve this, you must use both cold milk and a cold jug. If you are making two lots of foamed milk, then after your first round, cool your jug by rinsing with cold water before you prepare the second hot milk.

Trust me that this makes a difference, as you really don't want large bubbles of air in your milk foam, or your second foamed milk will be inferior to the first.

If you heat your milk to the optimal temperature and, only then, whizz it with a mechanical whirrer, then you will make large bubbles which will quickly disappear. This is what they call Macrofoam.

The only process that I have discovered which works well, is to use a milk 'wand' from an expresso machine to produce hot steam and insert this into cold milk in a cold jug. To start, dip it in and out a few times to introduce some air into the milk; then find the perfect steaming point, which is just below the surface of the milk and hold it there carefully, in order to create a vortex and this swirling air/milk mixture will create the perfect foam. As the level of foam rises, you must carefully raise the tip of your wand too, so that it is always just beneath the surface. Crucially, keep monitoring the temperature and stop at 65 degrees C, so using a milk thermometer is very important.

Interestingly, oat milk also contains the L Casei protein and foams beautifully in the same way as cow's milk. I have a light sensitivity to milk and prefer to make Oatachino at home using oat milk, and then sprinkle Belgian chocolate dust on the top. I know that sprinkling chocolate on cappuccino isn't traditionally Italian but I like it. I own about 30 different chocolate stencils which I sometimes use to make patterns on the coffee, depending on my mood and what is going on (Olympic themed, snowflakes, sunshine, etc.) This serves no practical purpose but makes me smile, so I would recommend trying it!

… and the key to perfect eggs?

If you want to make perfect eggs with a lovely, jelly-type consistency, then the important lesson is to start heating the eggs without agitating, which is totally the opposite to foaming milk. This is really important because you have to heat them slowly and wait until they start to solidify in the pan before agitating, since unlike foamed milk, you want to produce big bubbles. Then agitate them slowly with a wooden spoon and take them off the heat when they are almost cooked, since they will continue to cook for a short while afterwards.

I hope that you have great eggs and coffee from hereon.

If you are interested in learning more, then full instructions are on www.fullexperienceliving.com.

Olympic Coffee

§

Chapter 7.   University Years

Judge your success by what you had to give up in order to get it. Dalai Lama XIV

In life there are just two types of people – those who do the work and those who actually take the credit. Always try to be in the first group, as there is less competition there. Mahatma Ghandi

I started Keele University in 1987, with a complete fresh wardrobe of the latest fashion, including my beloved electric blue elephant cords and canary yellow cable sweater (this was the 1980s, remember!) and I was determined to have a good time and throw myself into student life.

I enrolled in lots of societies, since I wanted to reboot my life and leave the old Barry behind and figured that spreading my net wide would give me the best chance of finding a new friendship group.

I joined the Keele Rugby Club social society which, even then, seemed a strange thing to do, as I had hated playing rugby at school. One very strong memory was of me as a skinny 11-year old, standing on a cold, hard, rugby pitch with the freezing October wind blowing through my matchstick legs. Someone threw the ball at me. I caught it. After which twenty guys jumped on my head and I realised that rugby was definitely not the game for me. I never played rugby again and nor, seven years later, could I keep up with the frenzied beer-drinking pace of the Keele Rugby Club, so never returned to this either.

I also joined the Tolkein Society and didn't really fit there either (poor excuse for misfits to meet on a Monday night and drink beer) and also the Jazz, Funk and Soul society, at which, though I loved the music, I didn't feel like I belonged.

In the late eighties, all universities had a RAG society, which stood for 'Raising And Giving' and was a really important part of student life, existing solely to raise money for good causes. Sadly, they don't seem to exist anymore which is a shame, since it was excellent fun dreaming up new ways to raise money for good causes and none of us took ourselves too seriously.

I joined the Keele RAG committee in my first term and enjoyed the brainstorming of new ideas, project management and execution of these pursuits and above all, raising money to help people who were most in need. We were a team of about 12 people and as with all clubs and societies, just a few of us seemed to do most of the work but I didn't care. I let my mind race with developing new ideas to raise money and discovered that I was really good at both creative thinking and also organising. We attended the local town carnival and I instigated the idea to encourage visitors to throw their coins at us. I think that the element of danger that they might actually hit us with their money, encouraged more donations!

My crowning glory came in the summer of 1988, when we had already secured a donation of 300 condoms from Durex and custard powder from a local food producer that could make 3000 litres of custard. I had a brainwave when we unearthed an old bath which had been buried somewhere on our campus. My idea was that we could create our own version of the 1980s classic family gameshow, 'It's a Knockout' but the twist would be, that it would be based on custard-filled condoms!

I secured all the custard sponsorship, agreed permission from the university, designed the games and completely organised and promoted the event which took place on a sunny Saturday afternoon on the sports field. I remember that at the time, we had no idea whether anyone would turn up, or even if we would raise any money. However, happily it was a resounding success and also loads of fun and we even raised about £100. In case you are interested, a video of this event exists on YouTube of the three RAG weeks that I attended, which I have uploaded to www.fullexperienceliving.com for the highlights of this incredible day!

As an afterword, zoom forward 30 years and I was to revisit Keele University to take my son to start his degree – he had heard all of my stories and wanted to experience them himself! We met someone working at the gym who had started there back in 1988 and actually remembered our custard-condom sports day, though he also told me that this had been a one-off event, never to be repeated again. I guess that some ideas just have their time.

I also recall that we would visit other universities to sell our annual 'RAG MAG'. This was a booklet filled with the most smutty, racist and offensive jokes that we could find and the more shocking they were, the better! No one was above being made fun of and we loved that. We would design the small RAG MAG booklet in the summer before the academic year started and arrange for thousands to be printed. Our goal was to sell them throughout the year in order to raise money and it pretty much goes without saying, that writing a booklet to sell, which intentionally insults every race, religion, sex and pretty much every one else, could not exist today, so it is perhaps not that surprising that RAG as a concept has fizzled out.

Joining our regular visits to local towns and communities, I became our number One RAG MAG seller for 1987 by creating a unique method of selling them. One of the headline charities which we supported that year was BIBIC which existed to help brain-injured children. The method I dreamt up would be to spot unsuspecting shoppers and first catch their eye, then, as they approached me, ask them if they wanted to help brain-injured children and then wait for them to donate into my charity box - after all, how could any self-respecting member of the human race say no to that request?

I also threw myself into student politics and would often attend student union meetings to speak out against the injustices of the world. It is really hard to believe this in present times of government austerity, but in 1987 I had been awarded a full student grant and this meant that both my university course was free of charge, and I was actually *paid* to study. Privately, I thought this was grossly unfair but I like solidarity and also wanted to attend a really huge march, so I attended the 1987 NUS student march in London, to protest against the cutting of the student grant anyway.

I had another crazy idea in my first year too of running for Student Union President. Even though I knew that I had no chance of success, my strategy was to encourage people not to vote for me and use this to raise money for RAG. My idea was that I asked students to sponsor me for the number of votes that would eventually lose by - and it worked. There was an advertising character for Bassets Liquorish Allsorts at the time called 'Bertie Basset', so my slogan had been, "Sponsor Bertie for RAG and vote for someone else!" I did lose conclusively and I do remember that strangely, I still managed to garner 28 votes and raise about £30, so it was worth it and was fun too!

We had a small, tight circle of friends and we spent most of our time together, socialising, drinking tea, learning how to make roast dinners, Yorkshire puddings, mixing cocktails, visiting the union and attending the many annual student balls throughout the year. We looked after one another and gradually, turned into the people that we would eventually become. Over time, I also grew in self-confidence and my mind started to think about life and career beyond Keele. This is a scary concept for a 20/21-year old and frankly, at the time I was clueless.

Mobile phones would not exist for another decade, so calling home became a weekly ritual and since there were so few public telephones on campus, I had to queue for half an hour to wait for one of the five payphones at the Union building to become free, in order to speak to Mum and Dad. As my final year came closer, things back at home were not going well.

In 1988, Videomania had moved from the Neasden retail shop into a professional 3,500 sq. ft. industrial unit in Golders Green in North West London. My parent's thinking was that by moving into a more professional premises, their quality of customer and profitability would improve and they would make more money. However, their fundamentals of the business didn't change, so instead what happened was that their overheads went up and they started to lose money.

It didn't help that Dad was totally consumed with his editing business and he spent much of their first-year there learning how to weld, so he could build an edit console which looked like the professional edit suites of the West End Edit Houses, only without the cost.

During these calls, Mum burdened me with her fears for the business's escalating financial situation and she did this with floods of tears. Once she actually pleaded for me to leave my university course so that I could return home and help them to turn things around. Happily, my then girlfriend persuaded me to see sense and to remain at university in order to finish my degree and for that I am truly grateful to her.

I threw myself into mathematics during my final year and was determined to do well. At the end of a very long year and extremely tough exams, I graduated with a 2:1 single-honours degree in mathematics, specialising in nonlinear differential equations and later found that I had been just 2 percent short of achieving a first-class degree. However, since we used to tell ourselves that people who achieved firsts couldn't have had much of a social life, besides which by then I couldn't do anything about it anyway, I eventually came to terms with my disappointment.

After finishing my exams, I had an entire week free from studying before result's day and the annual RAG week-fest of an entire week of partying where anything goes. During this week, I picked up a book on what was then a brand-new branch of mathematics called *chaos mathematics*. From the first page I was hooked and discovered that this new subject built upon my favourite subject of non-differential equations and which underpins the entire mathematics of clouds, tsunamis and stock exchange prices.

I was totally mesmerised by this exciting new subject and for a few days, seriously considered embarking on starting a three-year PhD, in order to become a Chaos Mathematician, however, by this stage I was sick of being poor and ready to start the next chapter of my life.

Since there was an offer open for me to join the family firm and I was both young, willing and available, I thought that could do this for a few years, so what did I have to lose?

Quite a lot as it turned out.

PART II

Chapter 8.   Joining the family firm

Do not pray for an easy life, pray for the strength to endure a difficult one. Bruce Lee

Immediately after leaving university, I went on a three-week driving tour of Germany with my then girlfriend before starting work at Videomania Ltd but as soon as I did, I worked tirelessly to turn the company's fortunes around.

I have always been fascinated that the Trojan culture of 1,000 BC had such a deeply engrained work ethic, that 3,000 years later, people who work with extraordinary intensity and ceaseless energy are still being compared with them and this is exactly how I worked when I started working at the family firm.

Videomania in 1989 was a mess. The majority of its revenue was generated by buying job-lots of used video equipment from closing-down TV departments at clearance rates and then disposing of the choice items at premium prices. Of course, this meant that there was lots of stuff left behind, which by 1989 was piled 1.5m high in a large room and nobody had any clue where anything was. They didn't know what they owned, so they couldn't sell it and the pile simply grew higher and higher.

Buying and selling was handled by Mum and assisted by Ahmed, who also ran the service department. The workshop had half-finished repairs piled up onto all available shelves and work surfaces.

The edit suite was Dad's domain and looked extremely impressive. It gave the impression of being like the bridge of a spaceship. He had built a custom workbench which spread in a stylish semi-circle around his chair and included lots of devices with flashing lights and LED displays inset into the elegant grey plastic worktop, which were necessary to create visual effects and edit pictures in the 1980s. A bank of monitors was placed at eye-level behind the main console on another custom frame.

I still remember Dad telling me that the optimal viewing distance to watch a screen is 1.5 times the diagonal image size and to this day, our TV at home has screen dimensions which have been carefully calculated to be ideal for our room and the sofa is placed a carefully measured distance away from the OLED panel, in order to follow his advice.

A closer look at the edit suite, however, revealed that the patch panels were not properly marked and the wiring actually changed from week to week, depending on how he had decided to rewire his edit suite. Cables were strewn across the room to facilitate temporary rewires. Under the raised podium where the clients were supposed to sit, was a huge collection of power tools, including two welding machines, as this was the main place where Dad kept them so that they were always accessible. In a word, his edit suite was disorganised and it never worked 100% right.

Also, being situated in unfashionable North West London rather than the West End, which was the epicentre of the TV Industry, or West London in proximity to the BBC, meant that attracting clients was also difficult. That Dad was the only editor capable of driving this edit suite, since everything about it was custom-built and in a constant state of change, meant that this was more of a vanity project than a business, and it would be many years before the editing department would make any real money.

The camera rental department was a small, messy room containing shelves with a couple of used tripods and a large cardboard box full of assorted cables, all tangled together into a great morass. The rental department when I joined didn't have its own dedicated rental stock, as the strategy at the time was to rent out unsold equipment from its sales stock and all rentals were administrated by a lazy young technician/driver.

It was clear from the outset that I meant business and Mr Lazy soon realised that his days were numbered, so he left the week that I started and his absence was not missed.

The firm now comprised of Mum and Dad, Ahmed who ran the engineering department, a receptionist, an elderly lady who prepared the accounts and me.

Being aware that I was the owners' son and not wanting to be accused of having won my position by nepotism alone, I insisted on being paid the lowest wage of everyone in the company, including the newly departed Mr Lazy, so I started working at Videomania in September 1989 on a salary of just £6,000 per year and I was hungry for success.

After three years of studying degree-level mathematics, I was very surprised when the first task set for me was to count the number of valves contained in several ancient cardboard boxes. Mum had bought a job-lot of them and amazingly had found a buyer as well, but before she could sell them, she needed to confirm exactly how many valves there actually were to sell. They were so old that the cardboard actually disintegrated when I touched it and as I counted them, I remembered wondering why on earth I had studied for 3-years, if this was the sort of thing that I would be doing from now on. Of course, I now know that life is very much what you make of it and that everyone has to start somewhere.

Ahmed had started with the company as soon as he had left polytechnic and had been close friends for years and the two families had even shared some summer holidays together. Since they were boys, Ahmed and his brother would spend the weekends at our home and Dad would teach them electronics, since unlike me, they were interested in anything technical. Ahmed had a casual, relaxed approach to work and in order to retain him with the firm, my parents had made him a Director, albeit one without any shareholding.

Dad fiercely guarded the ownership of the company and was never going to willingly relinquish even a small shareholding without a fight. However, this would cause rising tension between Ahmed and my parents over time, as he had always understood that he would eventually receive a shareholding as he had been with the company since the very beginning and when it became clear that no shares were ever going to be offered to him, he left under a cloud. His departure left the triumvirate of the three Bassetts remaining to run the firm and each of them had their own ideas of where they were heading.

When I joined, it was made clear to me that my role would be to run the hire department, though in practice, it also meant doing all of the driving, collecting and dismantling equipment, invoicing, taking orders and pretty much anything else that needed doing. On the rare occasions when they were asked by clients to do any filming, I would assist camera and using my wedding experience, even operate camera sometimes too. In spite of these pressures, I personally took-up the challenge of making the company more efficient and this meant clearing up and organising all of the old stock, which brought be into constant conflict with Dad.

Dad was a hoarder and hated throwing things that he considered to be of value away. Whenever I tried to throw something away, he would strongly object and tell me that this had once been a 'very sought-after item' and ought to be kept since it might one day come in useful... I remember him using this phrase every time that I tried to dispose of something but I felt driven to clear the junk room. My efforts were rewarded, as I would frequently find equipment that we didn't know that we owned and which Mum was able to turn into cash. This helped the company's recovery, so in spite of the constant arguing with Dad, I did not rest until every corner of the company was clear.

Unusually, the Golders Green building had been purchased freehold by my parents and whilst this was a great idea, their move coincided with a time of very high interest rates which made servicing both a mortgage and paying the high overhead costs very tough. In fact, interest rates in the UK between 1989 and 1991 were never below 10 percent (peaking at 15 percent on Black Wednesday, September 1992 during the crisis of Britain withdrawing from the European Exchange Rate Mechanism [ERM]). These were dark days for owners of freehold houses and buildings.

I had also hugely underestimated what needed to be achieved in order to make the company profitable and with no industry experience, I had first to prove myself before my ideas could be taken seriously. My parents were interested in my ideas but I wanted to take them into a new direction, since I had no interest in the buying and selling business that had generated profit for them in the past.

By this time, they had lost much of their early-won market and a lot more competition existed now from better capitalised dealers who offered a more professional service, so my primary goal became developing the hire department. I had correctly deduced that the hire department's success relied upon repeat business and was convinced that a well-run operation could be tremendously profitable.

However, my new investment ideas for the hire department took a lot of persuasion, so to begin with, the hire-department stock was built up extremely slowly as for a while, we continued to hire out unsold equipment, with mixed success.

I vividly remember one day searching frantically around the building for a JVC KY27 camera before being told that it had been sold. "…But Mr Kambo is on his way to us now to collect this camera for hire!," I lamented. I can't remember how I resolved this hire but I do recall that this experience was not unique and extremely embarrassing.

We did eventually start to invest in new equipment specifically for the hire department, and over time, both the client base and hire department turnover grew, but a lack of capital and funding meant that we were always limited to what equipment could buy. Strategically, this meant that we could not afford the premium broadcast cameras whose lofty price tags were beyond our reach. The early Videomania brand became perceived as being both 'cheap and cheerful' and also unreliable. It worked for a while but was not a great place to start building a brand from.

Guided by my parents, though without a mentor, any industry experience or formal business training, my early strategy was to buy cheap second-hand equipment and flight cases for the rental stock. Eventually, I realised the importance of presentation, so as we began to invest in new cameras, editing suites and camera accessories, we also branded the cases, labels and cabling to enhance our reputation, albeit at the lower end of the market.

In late 1993, the firm went through a re-branding exercise, since Videomania was a really 1970s consumer electronics name and not at all appropriate for the serious, corporate rental company that I wanted to build. My parents were adamant that they wanted to retain the Videomania name since they didn't want to alienate their existing clients who had always known them by that name, so we all compromised on the new name of VMI, which stood for Videomania International Ltd. A new logo completed the rebrand and we felt that this was more appropriate for a professional 'Facilities House'. To this day though, I am a bit embarrassed when clients ask me what

VMI stands for and I am reluctant to tell them but we can't run away from our history!

I remember that during this period, there was a government department called Business Link which existed to provide help and guidance for small firms. We accepted their help and one day, a consultant came to visit us. Dad and I met with him and sat in his office. He asked us some searching questions, many of which I hadn't properly considered, and we both discussed the strategies that we each wanted to adopt over the next five years and it was very clear in this meeting, just how different each of our goals were.

When I explained what I wanted to do, the consultant asked me to qualify this rationale and I remember answering, "Because I feel it in my gut." He replied that I was 'shooting from the hip' and should instead apply solid business analysis, reasoning and planning in all of my future decisions and I have never forgotten this lesson. He also looked squarely at Dad and informed him directly that in his opinion, I should be Managing Director, since only I offered the business the best chances of success in the future. As you might imagine, this was not well received.

The next period saw VMI transition from a sales company into a rental company and whilst the accounts showed almost nil revenue growth and non-existent profit for my first five years, the company did indeed change dramatically during this time, as declining sales were steadily replaced with growing hire revenue. By 1994, the transformation was complete and VMI had emerged to become a camera rental company.

Progress was painfully slow since I was constantly learning on the job, found conflict in every decision and the three Bassetts were always arguing. There were frequent tears, outbursts and door slamming and I can honestly say that this wasn't a great time in my life. However, I was determined to help my parents and my hopeless optimism gave me the confidence that it would only be a short time before I started my actual career and that I wouldn't have to wait long for things to really change.

Zooming briefly ahead, compound annual revenues would increase massively from 2 percent per year to 26 percent per year for five straight years from 1995 but you will have to wait and see what happened first.

Our home in North West London

Chapter 9.   Make your own opportunities

It's funny, the harder I practice those bunker shots, the luckier I become. Jerry Barber (Golfer)

I have always loved skiing and visiting new resorts and in the early 1990s, took the opportunity to try a week's skiing in the Carpathian Mountains with a good friend of mine.

At the time, Romania had only recently toppled its communist dictatorship to become a free country, albeit a really poor one and understandably, they were really keen to encourage tourists to come and bring sorely-needed hard currency with them.

Whilst we stayed at the top hotel in the best ski resort in the country, we still found it ridiculously cheap compared with London prices, so for a week, we lived like Kings.

One evening, as we waited to order dinner in the most exclusive restaurant in the resort, I noticed two elegant men seated on the opposite side of the opulent dining room about to eat. They were very conspicuously dressed, with one wearing a very grand military uniform decorated with a lot of medals and gold braid and the other, a smart uniform of some kind which I didn't recognise.

I like to experience new adventures whenever I can and decided that it might be fun to engage with these two gentlemen, so I spontaneously lifted my beer glass and loudly exclaimed, "We wish you good health, from the United Kingdom!"

At this point, they could have ignored us and there would have been no story to tell but instead, they invited us over to their table and we were to spend the rest of the evening and much of the early hours in their company. We found out that the heavily decorated soldier was actually the second-in-command of the Romanian army, and his friend was the chief prosecutor of the Romanian judiciary, and whilst we were impressed with them, surprisingly, they were equally chuffed to be dining with two western visitors who had travelled all of the way from London.

We had only just met these people and I chose to ask some very probing questions to try and better understand the country, such as, "How could it be right that as civil servants, they were eating in a restaurant, where a single meal costs more than a month's wages for a regular Romanian?" and "How can it be right that westerners are by law, allowed to jump the long queues at petrol stations?" but Mr Medals did not appreciate my tone.

"I am very important man," he declared. "I not speak with you – you are young boy!" whereupon he spoke to my friend for the rest of the evening, who was 10 years my senior.

Happily, I am a fluent German speaker and conveniently, so was Mr Prosecutor, so we dined and both friends spoke to only one of the two men and one of them in German, and after our meal we drank a lot of vodka.

Sometime later, I realised that we were the only diners in the large room. By this time, all of the other customers had departed and the waiting staff were patiently waiting for us to finish, but neither Mr Medals nor Mr Prosecutor seemed to be in any hurry to finish.

"They cannot ask me to leave," Mr Medals declared. "I am VERY important man!" So, we enjoyed their hospitality for a while longer and in the early hours, after we had all enjoyed a very convivial evening, they drove us back to our hotel in their staff Mercedes.

I like this story, since it shows that we can all make our own adventures happen and unless we take chances when they occur, then these potential opportunities will just pass us by and be gone forever.

No one would have been any the poorer, had I not decided to toast the two gentlemen but our lives were certainly enriched for having taken a chance and we shared a very enjoyable evening together as a result.

Chapter 10. My MBA years

It is the worst of all mistakes to do nothing when you can only do a little. Do what you can. Sydney Smith

By 1993, I was becoming both impatient at my lack of progress and also a bit bored with my life and whilst I still wanted to help my parents to sort out their business before starting my career, I also wanted to broaden my horizons, so I decided to study for an MBA.

Dad had always revered Imperial College and by late 1992, they had opened a business school in London, so I applied for a place on their Executive MBA course. I would continue working during the two and half year part-time course, mixing with executives from large companies and hopefully also learning how to run a big business. My hope was that I may also find a new direction for myself too.

It is worth mentioning that at this time, I was motivated and driven to be a rich man. Becoming a millionaire had always been my Dad's unfulfilled dream and my goal was to achieve this by 30, so gaining an MBA seemed a logical step for me.

Arriving at the recently opened Imperial College Management School, situated in a beautiful Edwardian building in South Kensington, I attended my interview with the head of department.

Looking back now, I didn't look like an obvious candidate. On being asked what daily newspaper I read, I replied that I didn't read any. In that case, what weekly news magazines did I read? I once again replied that I didn't read any of those, either. Peter, the head of the business school looked perplexed. He asked me further, "Then what news programmes do I watch? How do I keep up with current affairs?" I calmly responded that I didn't watch any news programmes, as I had no interest in current affairs.

At the end of the interview, Peter asked me if I had any questions and of course, I had several.

The arrogant Barry of the time asked why I should choose to pay the expensive fees of Imperial College, when for a fraction of the cost, I could instead attend a distance-learning course at Herriot-Watt University, to which a now very frustrated Peter retorted with, "Otherwise when you tell people where you won your MBA, they will answer, 'Herriot who?'!". It would take some time for me to lose this unattractive, conceited streak

Sitting opposite Peter for the 40 minutes of this interview, I had observed that he had been slouching for the entire time. The end of the interview had come and I just couldn't help myself and without thinking, blurted out, "Peter, I notice that you have extremely poor posture when you sit. Look after your back and your back will look after you!" I was so arrogant and clearly had no idea of when to keep my ideas to myself, though it would take some years of bumpy experiences for me to learn this lesson!

I think that perhaps the recession of the early '90s may have resulted in low applications for the MBA that year or maybe Peter may have liked my honesty and drive but whatever the reason, I was offered a place at Imperial College Management School which I started in the spring of 1993. Peter and I joked about the posture comment for the rest of my time there, after which he moved on to a different university and we never met again.

Studying for an MBA is hard work. We came to the business school every second Friday and just sitting down attending lectures from 9am until 6pm is both arduous and tiring. Of course, we would work at our regular jobs for the rest of the time and attempt to squeeze in the immense amount of reading and coursework during the little spare time left over and I was perpetually tired.

By now I had met Cheryl and we were a serious couple who wanted to settle down and buy a house together. We met at university but had only started seeing each other after I had left Keele. Spoiler alert – we would marry the following year and buy our first house too!

At the time though, although we didn't have much money, we did have an innovative idea to help us to save for our deposit. Dad's workshop had been torn down a long time ago and Mum had saved and planned to build an extension to extend her kitchen but Dad had had other ideas. What remained for several years was an eyesore of exposed dug foundations reminiscent of World War I trenches, and which were always waterlogged. I designed a ground floor flat, filled the trenches with concrete and within six months, Cheryl and I had moved into our brand-new home together.

Our flat was very small and the only place where it was possible to fit a desk in was our bedroom. I would rise early and spend the first hours of dawn studying, then we would have breakfast together and both go to our respective places of work. In the evening after dinner, I would return to my desk and study until 10pm and this cycle would repeat every day, so for the best part of three years, I had virtually no social life.

As an aside, I did all of my studying wearing a pair of really thick cotton Avirex jogging trousers, which were really comfortable and we called them my 'MBA trousers'. I wore them so much that by the time of the exams, there were holes in the seat and the misshapen legs were stretched like chevrons, which were really baggy at the knees. I accidently wore these to one of my MBA final exams and the others students were shocked at how weirdly I was dressed, although this seemed entirely normal to me!

The Exec-MBA cohort of 1993 became a close-knit group of 23 people but on the first day, we hadn't met each other before and were given the 'paper tower' task to perform. If you know this task, then you will know what is coming but we came to this cold and learned some really valuable lessons about teamwork.

Our task was to build a tower out of paper and we were given a small pile of broadsheet newspaper pages and an extremely small reel of sticky tape. We were placed into 'syndicate groups' of four or five for the duration of the course, collaborating on projects and tasks together which was an important part of the training. The instructions for our first challenge were very clear – we must spend the initial five minutes discussing and planning only and then build for the second five minutes. Our towers would be judged on both height and 'beauty' and that was it! The clock started.

As soon as the task began it was clear that we were all construction experts! We all had what we considered to be a valuable opinion, but despite several attempts, I simply couldn't (or wouldn't) be heard!

I had been a Lego genius in my younger days and knew all about structural integrity, triangulation and building stability into a model, but the group's consensus was that we should all roll the thin pages together, overlapping slightly, in order to make a very long tube. Then we should all rotate this tube vertically so that it could stand up in order to make a tall tower. This made no sense to me, as I was certain that it would surely bend and break. I tried very hard to explain this to the group but no one was listening.

So I gave up. I stopped objecting and did exactly what they told me to do, and of course the tower broke into two as I said it would. Now it is was my turn and I took over!

I explained that while time was now short, two of us should make a long tube which would be the tower, but that it should be thick and not too long; another two would make three smaller tubes to act as legs and together, we would build a triangulated structure to hold the tower together… Then just before the buzzer was heard, our tower was standing and whilst it was neither the tallest, nor the most beautiful, we had completed the task.

After the conclusion, we all conducted Myers Briggs personality tests and were taught about psychometrics and the roles that different people played in teams. Perhaps unsurprising for MBA students, three of our group (including myself), were in a collective group described as 'Major Generals'. This confirmed what we already knew about ourselves, which was that in a team situation, we always like to take charge.

What I didn't realise however, was that if we don't get our way and are knocked off our pedestal, then we can resort to sulking, which is exactly what happened to me. This lesson really helped me to appreciate the roles that people play in teams and I think that if you find yourself in a crisis, then you will be pleased to have a Major General in charge.

Over time though, I learned that the best way to run a team is to allow people to play to their strengths and this is only possible if the leader works as a conductor, rather than a General. Do this and you will achieve a happy, productive team. I did eventually learn the lesson that sometimes it is easier to go with the grain and blend-in, rather than insist on drawing attention to myself and standing-out.

Coming from a small company, I found the modules on Human Resource Management (HRM) really difficult but overall, it was the volume of work that I found hardest of all to cope with. Having a maths degree came in useful when we studied statistics which I found very easy and I volunteered to give private lessons to many of my peers in order to help them to pass this module and this helped me on my way to becoming a more-rounded person.

In the second year of the course, we visited New York for a week-long industrial placement to visit many leading US companies to see how they did business. We visited Sony Pictures and EMI music, then later Solomon Brothers and actually visited their trading floor which I found really exciting.

One day, when an event had been cancelled, I decided to take a personal tour of New York to see what it was really like for myself. In the same way that lots of Americans think that London is always foggy and England is always raining, I had only ever only seen images from Bronx and Queens showing derelict cars on fire and angry looking gangland members standing in groups on street corners, and I wanted to see what the real New York was like. I hired a taxi and spent the afternoon visiting these areas and sure enough, I saw that it was nothing like the images which I had seen.

Around this time, we were studying finance and banking on my course, and my intellectual enthusiasm had been reignited for the first time since discovering chaos mathematics some years before. I had discovered the then new financial instruments of derivatives. These were immensely complex mathematical tools which actually meant that instead of dealing with something tangible, like exchange rates, company shares, gold or coffee, instead you traded in *risk*. I don't want to get into the details of this now but one of my favourite books to explain the financial crisis which followed and the role that derivatives played in it, is described in Andrew Ross Sorkin's excellent book *Too Big To Fail*.

On the plane home, I made a monumental decision that I was going to leave VMI in the following year and would become a derivatives dealer… and live in New York.

Cheryl was really supportive, since I was clearly, totally committed to this plan, so on returning to VMI in September 1994, gave written notice to Dad that in nine months' time, I would be leaving the company. I was basically running it now and wanted to give them plenty of time to find a replacement but I felt that my short time at the family firm was up and it was finally time for me to begin my career.

§

Chapter 11. Achieving the impossible.

Sometimes the lesser-trodden path is lesser trodden for a reason

It had always been a childhood dream of mine to fly a model helicopter. When I left Keele, I told my friends that I planned to buy a helicopter kit and learn how to fly it but they all tried to dissuade me, explaining that model helicopters were too hard to fly. I asked them all whether they had had any experience of flying helicopters and they replied 'no' but just knew this to be true.

This was well before the days of the semi-automatic model drones that we have now and flying helicopters then was *very* challenging. Undaunted though, I wanted to try this out for myself, so I bought a used model helicopter and despite many attempts, never successfully flew it without crashing, so they may have had a point after all.

Returning from my US trip and informing my friends that I now planned to be an international derivatives trader, they again tried to dissuade me, explaining that bankers worked really long hours and besides, this was a really stressful profession. I asked them how many bankers they knew and they replied that they didn't know any but they just knew… I didn't know any bankers at the time either, so I would have to find this out for myself.

I was now 26 years old and too old to be considered for a graduate entry position, and without a finance/banking background, it would be doubly hard for any bank to even consider me.

I had two factors in my favour though. Firstly, I was in the closing stages of my MBA and would shortly start writing a thesis but hadn't yet committed to a subject. Were I to join a bank, then I would write a finance modelling thesis which attempted to outperform the market in an original way and this would help my marketability. Secondly, I had a lot of persistence.

Over four months, I wrote to 61 merchant banks in London and received 61 straight rejections – well I knew that this wouldn't be easy!

However, I had saved the largest and most successful merchant banks to apply to, until last. In my sights were Goldman Sachs and Solomon Brothers, and my mission became to persuade them to employ me and then move to New York.

Mindful that I still didn't know any bankers or indeed anyone who worked at either of these banks, I needed to do some homework. I thought that it would be a reasonable assumption that some bankers may occasionally choose to go to a bar after work and perhaps I could talk to them. I left work early one day and visited the offices of Goldman's in London's financial district, then turned around and walked back to the station, looking out for suitable places where I could try out my plan. I noticed just two bars; one was a bit scruffy looking and the other looked smarter, so I entered the smarter bar, bought a mineral water, sat at a table and waited to see who came.

From about 5.15pm a trickle of people arrived which slowly grew to a stream, peaking around 6pm before slowing down and finally abating at about 6.30pm. It didn't seem like bankers worked super-long hours after all, I thought.

Now I had to talk to some people, in order to find out what international banking is like as a job and to find a name in the recruitment department, though this is easier said, than done. If you work with a tight group of people and visit a bar together, then you are likely to be quite resistant to a stranger trying to cut into your group but this is what I had to do.

To begin with, the group that I had initially chosen was deeply suspicious of me, and thought that I might be a journalist but I persevered and eventually won their trust. We ended up having a nice time together and by the end of the evening I had learned more about working at the bank and most importantly, had the name of a gatekeeper in the recruitment department.

A few days later, I took a day off and again went to Goldman Sachs, though this time I wore a suit and brought my C.V. with me. At 9.30am I called them up from my mobile phone and asked for Mr Gatekeeper by name but was told that he was busy. I left my name and number for him and asked that he call me back. I called him again at 10.30 and was told that he was still busy and again, I left my name and number. I then continued to call at 11.30, 12.30, 1.30 and 2.30 and each time, this was met with the same response.

However, by 3.30pm he must have been so sick of me calling, that he did take my call and we had a chat and a few days later, he invited me to a meeting. Result!

At my first meeting, he realised that I wasn't a complete idiot (useful) and I was invited back two more times and each time, more senior Goldman people attended.

In the final meeting, the head of recruitment looked me squarely in the eyes and told me that although they liked me, they were not going to take this any further. The reason she gave was that they did not believe that I would leave the family firm and despite me trying hard to persuade them that I was totally committed to leaving, they remained unconvinced.

I used the same approach with Solomon Brothers and what do you know – I received exactly the same response from them too.

I guess that they are both number One for a reason because, as you will find out, I never left the family firm after all.

Time for Plan B.

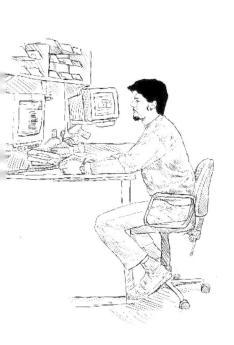

Camera floor of Golders Green Building, circa 1994

Chapter 12. Crunch time

Never be afraid to put your head into the mouth of the tiger…
anon

June 1995 was crunch time for me when I had to make a decision about whether I stayed with the firm to continue to help my parents, or left in order to start the banking career that I had planned for myself.

The timing was critical, as I had just four months until I my thesis deadline which, as we had been told, should take us at least 120 hours to complete. Forget about not having started it yet, I hadn't even decided on which subject or even, which field to base it on.

My MBA thesis would be a career-defining piece of work and I was conflicted. For me personally, it would have been better to have written some original finance-based research, which would have given me a unique specialism to help me to forge a career in banking. However, it was clear from my unsuccessful attempts of the previous six months, that I would first need to leave VMI and this would also carry some risk for me.

I was acutely aware that were I were to leave now, then the company was likely to go bust and my parents would lose everything. The past few years had seen some eyebrow-raising decisions from them and I could not see the company surviving in my absence. Once I had entirely cleared the junk room, they realised that this now large, clear space could be converted into a video studio, however, we had no experience of running a studio.

No matter though - Mum had bought a clearance job-lot of studio lights and also a lighting rig after a studio had closed down and they thought that by installing these in the space, they could then market a fully-functional studio.

Of course, this also meant further expense for the company, with extensive rewiring and needing to order custom-made black drapes as well. This plan had never been properly thought through, since the space was unusually small, with a low ceiling and both of these factors would limit its use.

We hadn't installed either a green room or changing rooms and these would both be expected when booking a studio as well. If that wasn't enough, the parking was very limited, which is a critical problem too, since crew and talent would usually drive. Unsurprisingly, it was rarely used and never proved itself to be financially viable, so after just a couple of successful jobs in three years, the studio was closed down and instead (and I am not joking), Dad used the space to store his 30ft boat, so that he could work on it during the day and in his spare time.

It wasn't all bad news since by now his edit suite had been moved upstairs and we now employed a staff editor and it was finally making money.

The major problem was, that since I had given written notice to Dad some nine months previously that I would be leaving the company, he had made no attempt to find a replacement for me, in spite of me reminding him every month to ensure that he took my plans seriously.

Monthly exchanges occurred between Dad and I and these were always terse and unconstructive and went something like this:

Me: "Dad, you know that I am leaving in eight-months' time, don't you?"

Dad: "Yes, of course I do".
"…but you haven't made any provision
to find a replacement yet!"

"I know, I know…"
He just didn't take the prospect of me leaving the company seriously
and this exasperated me.

By this time, VMI no longer bought and sold equipment any more, or
earned revenue from repairs. I was fully in charge of running the
camera hire department which was generating the vast majority of
company revenue with just a small contribution coming from the
editing department. It was my view that my parents simply didn't
possess the skills required to run the company that it had evolved
into.

We had a fleet of computer-based editing systems for hire, called
Shotlister and I alone was performing their installation and technical
support. I was also taking the majority of the camera hire orders
(using a magnetic board which I had made) and also preparing the
camera kits for hire with a single assistant. We were still a very
small company with an even smaller team but at the time, I was
involved in virtually every aspect of it and there was absolutely no
succession plan in place, in case I left.

The crunch time finally came on Friday 16th June 1995, when I
walked into Dad's office.

"Dad, I gave you notice of me leaving
VMI nine-months ago…"

"I have cleared my desk and I am about
to go on holiday for two weeks and I am
not coming back."

"OK. I am not stopping you from
leaving."

"Yes I know but I feel bad about going, since you haven't made *any* attempt to find a replacement for me.

"The company needs the implementation of a computer rental system; a new computer network; effective management team; better trained staff; staff motivational strategies; better quality control and improved reputation; a training strategy; a product market strategy; advertising and promotional strategy; it needs to be taken more seriously by its suppliers; improved capitalisation; a website so that we have representation on this new internet thing…"

"Above all, we need a five year strategic business plan…"

"The company needs all of this and the *only* person who can achieve all of these things, is me and I am leaving."

                    "If you want to leave, then I am not stopping you."

"…but I am conflicted. Whilst I have every confidence that I can make a successful career in the city, I couldn't live with myself if you and Mum lost everything because I left and the company subsequently went bust.

"I am also aware that you purchased the

freehold of the building to be your pension nest-egg for when the mortgage was paid off and if it went bust now, then you would lose this too."

[dramatic pause for this to sink in].

"However, I am prepared to stay…

…but only if I am made Managing Director and given a stake in the firm, since at the moment, I am just a salaried member of staff and am about to forego my career in the city."

[another dramatic pause]

"You *don't* have to do this, since I am now leaving VMI, having given you several months' notice. However, when I return from holiday in two-weeks' time, should you present me with a written offer to become VMI's Managing Director and with it, a third of company shares, then I will agree to return but I will only do so as MD."

On hearing this, Dad was ashen-faced but said nothing.

"I have one final demand," I said.

"Assuming that I stay, then for my MBA thesis, I plan to write a five-year business plan for the company and my goal will be to make VMI into a saleable going concern, so that I can sell the company."

"My plan is to receive a suitable price for VMI, so that we can buy an annuity, which will enable both you and Mum to be paid £50,000 per year for life, increasing with inflation."

"As well as giving you both an income, it will also give me an exit strategy, so that I can then decide *what* I am going to do after this chapter closes. What is certain is that if I stay now, then I will forego any chance for me to have a career in the city."

I then left his office to silence. He had only uttered a few words and I had dropped a bombshell on him, for which he would never forgive me.

Cheryl and I did enjoy our holiday on the Greek island of Aegina but always on the back of my mind was wondering exactly what was going on back in London.

Though I didn't know this at the time, VMI was collapsing like a house of cards.

Head of Accounts – "With Barry going, I don't want to stay. I'm leaving."

Mum – "…with Barry going, *I* don't want to run this company on my own."

"…Jeff, *if* you don't make him Managing Director, then I want a divorce."

So, I returned to VMI on Monday 3 July and Dad presented me with an offer letter which he had signed, inviting me to become Managing Director and which included a third share ownership in the company.

Whilst this is what I had asked for, I was always sad that he had never made me this offer with good grace and even years later, he would claim that he hadn't really made this offer to me at all. Instead, he felt that he had had a gun placed against his head, believing that he had been given no choice in the matter. I felt that this was really unfair and although I wasn't the one who was putting pressure on him to agree to this course of action, he would always blame me.

What was clear to me was that I was damned whichever decision I would make, and whilst I had only ever made this offer for reasons of safeguarding my parents' financial wellbeing, they never thanked me for it.

We have to live with the consequences of our decisions and things would not become much easier for me for a very long time.

Peter Zac in Edit 1, circa 2005

PART III

Chapter 13. Early years of being Managing Director

An optimist is a guy that has never had much experience. Don Marquis

And this mess is so big
And so deep and so tall,
We cannot pick it up.
There is no way at all!

Dr. Seuss. The Cat in the Hat

Dad had a small scruffy piece of paper roughly torn out of a shorthand notebook which was pinned to the wall of his workshop in pride of place by the entrance. The torn perforations were still affixed, and its curled edges would have given anyone the impression that this was just a scrap of paper because it looked insignificant in every way, entirely betraying the value of the solitary word which had been written upon it with a biro.

GODO

Even the word itself wasn't easily intelligible, being comprised of a mashup of two words, described elegantly in English to be a *portmanteau* of "Go" and "Do".

But GODO (pronounced GO-DO) was the mantra with which he aspired to live. It meant that if you wanted to achieve anything, then you simply got up and did it and this was something which, for his entire life, he had found very hard to do.

Mum would complain that there were many half-finished projects at home that Dad would start but never finish, and this really irritated her and I think that it irritated him too. Projects like the jumble of cables behind the TV in the living room, which had been part of his unfinished plan to route all video cables to the three bedrooms upstairs and also to his workshop; or the exposed trenches outside their home, which had been waiting for three years to be filled with concrete in order to turn it into foundations for a proposed new extension that Mum had dearly wanted. These were the same foundations onto which we would build our first apartment when I left university.

This was GODO at work and the word implied a value which Dad always admired in me. He may have used it as often as he did, perhaps because he believed that the magic of its implied meaning might enter him, somehow causing him to procrastinate less.

I love the famous Chinese proverb, from the Dao De Jing ascribed to Laozi:

A journey of a thousand miles begins with a single step

Now, I had a major project to totally turn the company around, shed half of the existing people and employ new ones, design and implement a new strategic direction and write a new business plan. I had to do this quickly because the deadline for my thesis submission was less than four months away.

I had worked very hard before, but now I worked like a man possessed, as there simply were not enough hours in the day to write my thesis in the spare time that I had. It also didn't help that our busy-busy season started in September, which coincided with an annual video convention in Amsterdam which we always attended called IBC, and would lose me a very valuable weekend.

So, I trained myself to survive on just six hours sleep and now woke an hour earlier at 5am and went to bed an hour later at 11pm, in order to give me a fighting chance of squeezing everything in.

Reading my thesis all of these year later, I wrote that:

> 2002 has been chosen to be the year that VMI will have an option of being sold and the three Directors going their separate ways. Shares will be split three ways in a ratio of

35:35:30. It has been discussed that in order to retire comfortably, my parents will require a lump sum of £900,000 in six years. This is equivalent to an annuity paying £50K/year for life increasing at 2% per year (prudential estimate). The inclusion of my shares and administration costs of selling the business which have been estimated at 10%, calculates an implied value of £1.4m.

Since our accountants had valued VMI back in 1995 to only be worth around £250K (and most of this value had been due to the increase in value of its freehold building), my goal became to increase VMI's value by 560 percent in just six years and then selling it.

This would be a tough challenge by any measure but Dad didn't make this any easier for me. My new title of Managing Director didn't help me to make decisions much quicker than before, since every piece of marketing material that I would design and each new appointee that I would interview, would need to be critically scrutinised by him. I often didn't agree with him either and when neither of us backed down, this made for some really unpleasant times.

We made progress nonetheless and 1995 saw rapid growth in in the company, as we invested in more of the latest AVID computer-based editing systems which were starting to become popular and continued to increase our rental camera inventory to keep up with growing demand.

Crucially though, we needed both a new strategic direction and to simultaneously reposition ourselves from 'cheap and cheerful, also-ran', into a rental company with a real USP (Unique Selling Point) - something which is very hard to achieve.

I first heard the news, at the IBC broadcast equipment convention in September 1995, that both Sony and Panasonic were planning to launch entirely new digital formats the following year. I realised that this would revolutionise TV production and provide the key to the new rebrand that I was looking for, for the company. The timing was perfect. At this exhibition, Sony had announced that they would be introducing a new digital video format called DVCAM for release in 1996.

My business plan would feature a major investment of these cameras and my idea was to approach Sony directly and persuade them to agree to a VMI/Sony joint-marketing proposal, which would both improve our market positioning and also help Sony increase awareness of their new technology. Then, when the equipment landed in late 2006, with Sony's help of early allocation and preferential pricing, we would be ready to capitalise on it.

It was a gutsy move but I felt that the timing was right, though I needed to improve so many things at the same time and also persuade a major manufacturer to work with us, that success was by no means assured.

The market research which I had completed for my thesis had confirmed that staff, quality control, presentation and a good range of equipment were critical success factors when people choose a rental company, and I was acutely aware that at the time, VMI was weak in every one of these areas.

I pulled it off though and submitted my thesis, graduating with an MBA in early 1996 at a ceremony held the Albert Hall and then in April that year, visited LA for the biggest, annual, international video convention called NAB, where I would present my marketing plan.

Visiting NAB for the first time, I had prepared a fully comprehensive business proposal for Sony to consider, so that VMI would be given early allocation to buy £250,000 of the latest new digital equipment. In return, Sony would engage in a joint marketing campaign with VMI to launch this new format.

A fully-costed marketing campaign included posting full page ads in all of the colour broadcast journals, and also booking the Planet

Hollywood restaurant in London for an entire day of presentations. I estimated the marketing alone would cost £40,000 and had asked Sony to contribute £20k of this.

Just in case they said no, I had also prepared an identical proposal for Panasonic, replacing the words *Sony* with *Panasonic* and *DVCAM* with *DVCPRO*, which was their version of the same format!

VMI at the time was a complete nobody in the market and I was really nervous when I gave my presentations but incredibly, both Sony and Panasonic accepted my proposal, so I committed to working with Sony and the plan was put into motion.

Everything went like clockwork that year which included another rebranding of VMI, employing a new team and implementing new measures and procedures to help increase our quality standards.

While this was happening, I also employed a new person to manage the DVCAM marketing plan and surprisingly, everything went to plan and the launch event, which was held at Planet Hollywood restaurant in October, was a roaring success with 400 industry visitors attending!

As is common with new equipment launches, delivery dates for the new equipment were pushed further and further back and now, having launched these brand-new professional cameras, clients rang us on a daily basis to hire them but Sony could not confirm a delivery schedule. October became November, then December... In fact, the cameras wouldn't be fully available to hire until late January 1997, which coincided with the only Japanese factory which manufactured the new DVCAM tapes, burning down, so in fact, the format wasn't properly available to use until April 1997, some six months after my event.

This could have been a disaster but an unintended consequence of my marketing, was that I had managed to reposition VMI to be the premier London rental company to stock the new, small, digital cameras for hire, which used the consumer version of the DVCAM format, now called DV. Sony's new DV camera was a hit with everyone from MTV to the BBC and overnight, everyone seemed to be using them. Our little company became the automatic rental company to call if you wanted to rent one.

At just £3,000 per camera, we were buying these five at a time out of cashflow and they had a rapid payback of just a few months, compared to the industry payback estimated to be just over two years, according to my thesis. Before long, we had 30 of these in stock and were building a really profitable business and revenue took off.

The period from 1995 to 1999 saw the company generate half a million pounds of clear net profit. Annual revenue would triple from £0.5m to £1.5m per year in 1999, as the company had enjoyed five straight years of 26 percent compound growth and was now in the best shape that it had ever been in. This same period had seen us taking part in joint-marketing initiatives with Sony, Panasonic, AVID, Canon and JVC, all of which had markedly increased the visibility of our brand, as VMI's reputation grew. The company also won three industry awards, including Hire Company of the Year (1998), Broadcast Hire Company award (1999, which was the only year that it was run) and the Natwest award for good business practice (1999).

The edit business had also become quite strong and by late '99, VMI rented out some 20 AVID editing systems and the edit business which Dad had started, now included a second edit suite, employed two staff editors and had its own branding of VMI Digital. Every year saw VMI becoming stronger and this had not escaped the attention of its competitors. Suddenly in 1998, three years ahead of the plan, a competitor approached VMI and made us an offer to buy the company outright for £1.5m.

The aim had been to sell the company for £1.4m but would the founding Directors now honour their promise to sell?

Err… sadly not.

The author with early DVCAM Camcorder

Chapter 14. It's not fair

Men in general are quick to believe that which they wish to be true. Julius Caesar

Back in 1998 and '99, I wasn't even thinking about a trade sale for VMI – things were much too busy and hectic at work.

The company was growing and we operated a staff of about 20 people. We always seemed to be employing new people and building more divisions, so I was busy growing a management team to ensure that the firm could transition from one-man-band to professional corporate entity.

The company was now organised into five departments including a Rental Desk which took phone calls and rental bookings; Camera Floor which prepared and returned the camera hires; AVID department which hired out mobile computer-based edit systems; VMI Digital which managed the two in-house edit suites and also the Accounts department. Each had its own Head of Department and all were fairly young and inexperienced. We would occasionally meet altogether at management meetings which I would chair, and my parents who didn't properly fit into any of these teams would also attend. We still argued frequently and this would sometimes happen in these meetings or in the office with others present, which was very embarrassing for me. Door slamming, raised voices and tears would regularly punctuate the air and it often didn't feel like I was working in a professional organisation at all.

The hire department was still responsible for the majority of company revenue, and whilst I now had an assistant to help take orders and a team of technicians preparing and returning hire orders, I was still involved in every major decision and working with Dad continued to be difficult, since I would do all of the work and the planning and then he would then criticise me.

Mum was still very much involved in the day-day running of the company and took care of all of the leases, paying the bills, looking after the staff and housekeeping. She also helped to take some rental orders when it was really busy and although she was not very organised, we supported each other and worked together well for most of the time.

Dad was officially the chairman of the company, who spent much of his time sitting in his office. He helped to repair things which were damaged, and gave the technicians some technical training which was appreciated, but he adopted quality control to be his focus. This was one of the critical success factors that I had prioritised in my business plan.

He spent much of his time checking kits which were ready to be collected and had a special 'quality checked' stamp which he would use to stamp job sheets in order to demonstrate our commitment to excellence. I remember that he would inspect a kit and verify that every battery supplied was showing 5 bars of power which meant that they were 100 percent charged. This was helpful, although he wouldn't ensure that essential cables were present if they had not been previously requested, so kits might still have errors even if they had passed his quality-control. His intentions were always good but he was never able to give me the support that I really needed and our relationship was testy.

The company worked well but it was frantic, with constant firefighting and frayed nerves. Emergency deliveries were an everyday occurrence to rectify orders which had experienced issues, so as a result, there was relentless stress at work. The business was continually changing and growing and our technicians were not well-trained because at the time, the company didn't pay well and so staff retention was poor. This was another of my early errors, which we have happily rectified now.

I remember that Golders Green was a really pressured place to work and I would be frequently inundated with demands from various members of staff who looked to me first to solve their issues. Every day I would receive calls from techs who couldn't find cameras on the shelves, or to notify me that essential accessories were damaged or incomplete and I was expected to rectify this by magic! This was often because we had not put equipment away correctly, or due to untidiness or not fully resolving previously incomplete returns. The company did work but it never worked like a well-oiled machine, which was a source of considerable frustration for me.

Cheryl recalls that every six months, I would come home with my head in my hands and lament that I simply couldn't do this anymore, since I just didn't have the support at work that I needed. Then we would have a heart-to-heart talk when she would (helpfully) suggest that I leave the company and start a career elsewhere. Every time though, I would end up returning to VMI, like a wounded warrior, returning into the throes of battle! As least that is how it felt to me.

I did attempt to hire and train department heads to be able to autonomously run their departments, but my parents would continually undermine their authority and thus sabotage my efforts, so they never stayed for very long.

So, when we received our first offer to sell VMI back in 1998 and then, amazingly a second offer a year later, my heart leapt, since this offered me the way out that I had been working towards.

This would be my freedom to really do what I wanted and I could finally leave VMI!

Immediately, Cheryl and I worked out our finances and decided that we needed a plan. Aware how important I still was to the firm, I assumed that I would need to commit to another two years to the company since any buyer would expect this, in any potential sale.

My son Josh, was also due to be born in September 1998, so we made the perhaps less obvious decision, that we would become tax exiles for two years and tour Europe in a luxury caravan. We were so serious about this, that we had already selected and spec'd out our caravan, paying extra for air conditioning and bike rack options and had even paid a deposit to reserve one, so that we could collect it once the company had been sold.

However, this did rely on my parents agreeing to sell the company and at the time, it didn't occur to me that they might renege on their promise. On receiving the first offer to buy the company from an industry conglomerate, I attended the initial meeting and agreed basic terms, then reported back to my parents with the good news.

You would have expected them to be happy! Videomania in the ten years before I had joined, had never made any profit or paid them well either. In fact, in 1998, the year that we received the first offer to buy the company, VMI was performing so well, that it had generated 35 times the average level of profit of the 10 years before I had joined. This sale, just three years after I had become MD, would give them both an exit and a £50K guaranteed annual income for life, yet they both looked very glum.

Mum had been impressed by the company's stellar growth and expected that this would continue in the future, and wondered whether it was the right time to sell after all. She reasoned that if we waited just a few more years, then the company would be worth so much more, so her decision was that we should not accept this offer.

Dad however countered with a phrase that I will always remember. "Barry, I have still so much to give. I am just not ready to retire yet."

It was extremely clear to me that they would not sell – not now and not ever. With just a third of the shareholding, I had no power to make this happen, so had no choice but to return, so return I did.

When the second offer to buy the company was received in 1999, it was met with the same response. It seemed that I was the Goose which proverbially laid the Golden Egg and they had no intention of setting me free.

At this time in my career, I couldn't put a foot wrong with the company and whatever ideas I had had, they seemed to be successful. Manufacturers liked my energy and originality and the company had a growing reputation in the marketplace. Although VMI was still small, we were doing interesting things and it continued to make money and grow and I was the driver to all of this.

I had another original idea too: Since I spent most of my time on the telephone, in front of a computer, I deduced that if I couldn't leave VMI, then I might as well make a lifestyle decision to move out of London and run the company remotely. I would still have a telephone and a computer, just live somewhere pretty to bring up my son.

You will guess that my parents would not support me with this decision either and for this, we would all pay a very hefty price.

I later found out that the second offer that we had received to buy VMI had come from a Group who at the time, also owned the UK's largest drama camera rental business (and which by some coincidence, my later business partner, Kevin, was a director of). Three years later they messed up their business and promptly went into receivership, so perhaps in retrospect, selling was not the right decision for VMI after all, though at the time it definitely felt like the right one to me.

I wouldn't be leaving VMI now and I was about to embark on the hardest ten years of my life.

Chapter 15. A lifestyle choice

Remember, happiness doesn't depend upon who you are or what you have, it depends solely upon what you think. Dale Carnegie

The new Millennium was fast-approaching and I was impatient to start the next stage of my life.

The 2000 financial year would see VMI's revenue increase by a massive 26 percent (which by coincidence was the average rate of growth for the previous six years too) and by now we had fully established our edit facility, VMI Digital into a proper going concern. It had been recently relocated from unfashionable Golders Green to its own building at a chic location in West London close to the BBC. The facility now had capability for expansion beyond the two main edit suites and was now under the expert management of Peter Zac, who had joined us a couple of years previously as a skilled Editor. This new move was an excellent decision, since under Peter's management, the post-production business really flourished and continues to exist today as an independent edit facility called West Digital, which both Peter and his partner, Darren still run.

VMI had acquired a 'crewing division' in 1999 by buying the goodwill of a company called Crystal Television which had just closed down. This gave us a functioning filming department, which managed five separate camera teams (crews) which were contracted to supply the Granada TV network with news footage for their primetime, daily news programme, *60 Minutes with Trevor McDonald*.   After acquisition, this illustrious contract transferred to VMI and was really important to us, since the department shared much of our existing camera fleet, avoiding the need for us to buy too much equipment and this increased our revenue markedly. For the first couple of years, it operated out of a different building which was just a few miles away from us and managed by two big characters, Margaret and David. The symbiotic relationship of VMI Crews and VMI worked really well – at least to begin with.

Our AVID department which rented out the mobile edit suites, was run by another big character called Dado. My policy has always been to allow key members of staff to create their own job titles and Dado became VMI's first and only *AVID Wizard!* I remember interviewing Dado for the role, which involved working a lot of unsociable hours to perform installations and providing technical support. I asked him how he would cope with the workload, since I explained, the previous department head had frequently sent me emails at 3am to ensure that I knew he was still working. Dado answered me confidently that he would ensure that the systems that were built by him were sufficiently reliable, that he wouldn't receive calls at 3am because the systems wouldn't break down – and he was right!

VMI's growing rental business continued to buy more cameras for its growing fleet and every year saw new digital formats released by various manufacturers and 2000 was no exception.

Panasonic had announced that they planned to release the DVCPro 50 format and we considered this to be a brave move, as they aimed to challenge Sony's Digital Betacam format, which at the time was universally used in mainstream production. Manufacturers had to be very gentlemanly in their approach to marketing in the UK, and felt that they could not make direct comparisons between technologies and equipment from different vendors, but I was independent and could be much freer in my approach.

I proposed a very aggressive marketing proposal to Panasonic which would include a strong graphic image of a pair of gloves with the DVCPro 50 logo pitted against another with the Digital Betacam logo, and this would be styled as a fight in a boxing ring with the words "You Decide!" printed underneath. I planned to shoot blind tests of both formats and send these to chief engineers at BBC, ITV and Channel 4, who of course, would not be able to tell the difference between the formats and would have to report their conclusions confirming this. Panasonic gave me the green light, so the test shoot went ahead and the broadcast engineers wrote their reports.

A big story about the comparison test appeared in a major industry journal, which included the engineers' statements confirming that they could not tell the formats apart, and this edition include full-page display adverts inviting visitors to my event. We hosted this at the Hard Rock Café and it was well attended by key industry delegates who were able to scrutinise identical recordings from both formats, side-by-side on matched monitors. No one attending was in any doubt that DVCPro 50 was indeed as good as Digital Betacam!

It was great for VMI and Panasonic and kept developing VMI's reputation for being ahead of the curve and doing interesting things.

My big move, however, was to find and employ a new manager to act as my second-in-command at the company, to allow them to effectively run VMI if I were to take a back seat. Once this person was installed and trained, I would be free to move out of London to start a new chapter in my life.

It took me three months to find Warren, whom I was confident would be a perfect individual to run VMI in my absence. This would be a first for the company, so when he needed a company car, we bought him a new Mercedes, which was another first as well. It took me six full months to train him, so that all of my systems could continue when I left.

I worked hard and wrote an entire quality manual, which I bound and distributed to all staff and Heads of Departments of all of the processes and procedures for the company, so that everyone in the company would have access to a set of SOPs (Standard Operating Procedures) to follow. This was a tremendously detailed document and included procedures of all company functions of all departments, from taking an order, to raising an invoice; from raising a crew, to returning an AVID system and from performing a data import to making a daily backup.

By now, I had promoted one of the client contacts to Rental Desk Manager, and with the addition of the new crewing division, VMI was now a strong company with six independent departments.

My goal was that with a structured management team in place and all activities proceduralised, including training and recruitment, I was now finally able to adopt a hands-off approach and run the company from a distance.

It had always been a goal of ours to build our own house and at last we had an opportunity to do so. We just needed to decide where our new home should be.

Having been mostly privately educated which had given me a great start, I planned this too for my son. At the time, a full private education cost circa £200K but though most of the excellent state-run grammar schools had been closed during the 1980s, a few still remained in Lincolnshire and Kent and were as good as the best private schools. I found out later that there were also some remaining in Buckinghamshire which would have suited us much better than Kent but we stupidly ignored these. We realised that if we moved to an area which was within the catchment area of a top grammar school, then we could a live in a beautiful rural place and send our son to be educated at a top grammar school and it wouldn't cost us a penny.

We had ruled out Lincolnshire early-on as being too flat and so decided on Kent. I held onto an early idea that I wanted to live on a hill in order to avoid the risk of flooding, which was quite prescient for the time. We took a map of Kent and drew a red ring around all towns which included a top 100 grammar school and spent an entire weekend visiting every one, so that we could decide where we wanted to live and in doing so, shortlisted Tonbridge and Cranbrook, before settling on Cranbrook.

Now, we needed to find a plot, however these only came up rarely for sale, since UK building restrictions made building new custom houses a rare event. However, I was never one to be worried about a challenge, so we searched and eventually, found a plot for sale in Benenden which was within the grammar school catchment area.

When we visited it however, it proved to be disappointing, quite expensive and borderline not cost-effective. We were so desperate to move, that we decided to make an offer anyway. On walking to the Estate Agent to make our formal offer, we happen to glance at the window of another Estate Agent on the same road and noticed the details of the house that we now live in. Again, the property wasn't ideal but we saw tremendous opportunity of the house that it could become. We viewed it that afternoon and made an offer which was immediately accepted.

The following week we accepted an offer to sell our own house and the sale went through really quickly. We agreed to complete and moved in just eight weeks later.

What possibly could go wrong?

Chapter 16. Fast food for cows

Never try to teach a Pig to sing – it wastes time, won't work and annoys the Pig. Anon

I have always had a lot of ideas and often tell people that I have around 20 original ideas per day, at which point my Co-Director, Kevin retorts that usually, 18 of them are rubbish!

He is quite right of course but you have to have fresh ideas first, in order to spot the ones with real potential to change the world.

I read once that:

Nirvana is the feeling that you have, between having a great idea and… discovering what is wrong with it

I don't remember who said this but it resonates very well with me!

Dad and I would relish challenging conventional thinking and discovering new ways of doing things which hadn't been considered before.

Our home in Kent overlooks a field which is rented by a local farmer. When we first moved here, Josh aged 2, would come down to breakfast each morning and always say good morning to the sheep who at the time lived in the field.

Then for many years the field lay fallow, until one day when we received a letter from the landowner informing us that he now planned to keep stock in the field. Coming from a corporate background, I was horrified to picture pallets and crates spoiling our view and when I called him, this was received with laughter, as the owner answered that *obviously* he had meant livestock. We would soon have cows living in the field!

Over the next ten years, we became quite used to seeing cows from our home and then one day, I had a unique idea – people like fast food, so what about cows?

Cows have three stomachs and a specially adapted digestive system to be able to survive on an exclusively grass diet, ruminating for hours chewing the cud and enabling them to digest cellulose-based food.

I wondered whether grass clippings could be their version of fast-food?

I tried to persuade them to eat the clippings from my lawnmower and to begin with, they were deeply suspicious and were frankly, very slow learners. Eventually though, one cow finally understood and tasted what I had been trying to persuade them to eat. From the gusto with which she tucked into the grass, it was clear that she preferred the clippings of the choicest fresh new growth from my neat lawn, rather than the rough weeds and mature woody growth of the poorly tended field. The other six cows soon joined in and in a very short time, all were heartily eating the lawnmower clippings that I had provided for them.

Each time thereafter that I would cut my lawn, I would throw my clippings into the field next to my house and in just a short time, the cows would come running (literally!) to my wooden fence to eat this tasty treat.

It didn't take them long for them to associate the noise made by my petrol-powered mower with the promise of a tasty snack, so in true Pavlovian spirit, as soon as I would start the engine of my mower, began a cacophony of mooing which could be heard from the field next to my garden. Unfortunately, they didn't distinguish between the sounds of my mower and those of our neighbours' mowers, so each time anyone in the vicinity would cut their grass, the cows would all simultaneously start loud synchronised mooing until they were fed. I then had to instruct all of my neighbours to tip their clippings into the field adjacent to my house, in order to keep the cows happy, which they were happy to do!

Then one day, the farmer who rented this field moved the cows to a new location and though I never found out where they this was, I did sometimes ponder on how quizzical their new neighbours must have been when, upon mowing their grass, they would suddenly hear the loud mooing music of the cows which used to live next door to us…

Chapter 16. A horrible year

It is easy to dodge our responsibilities, but we cannot dodge the consequences of dodging our responsibilities. Josiah Stamp

I recall a joke which depicts a man standing on a volcano which is showing clear signs that it will explode very soon. Three cars stop to offer him a lift as they evacuate to a safer place but he politely declines, claiming that God will save him. A military vehicle also stops and requests rather more forcefully that he join them to escape but once again, he declines their offer. Lastly, a helicopter scouring the area for potential evacuees, pleads that he must join them or he will be surely be killed, though as before, he once again insists that God will save him and remains standing on the now, very angry volcano. The volcano explodes and inevitably he dies, after which he rises to the pearly gates of heaven where is he is greeted by St Peter and God. He implores to God, "Where were you in my hour of need?" God replies, "I sent you three cars, a military vehicle and a helicopter, what more did you expect…!"

I dwell on this apocryphal story, as Cheryl and I were about to leave our home in very convenient Hertfordshire which was situated just a 20-minute drive to work and where we were also close to friends and family. Our plan was to move 100 miles away to a rural idyll but which would instead require a two and a half hour commute to work by car, train and tube *each way*. It was a poor decision, driven perhaps by a well-considered strategy but one that was fundamentally flawed and although we both had our own personal doubts about our plan, we did not choose to share them with each other.

We were running away from the company *and* my family, since I felt trapped and despite working extremely hard, could not see a way out, so the Kent plan was put into motion.

What resulted over the next 12 months was interdepartmental war and the business spiralling to near-bankruptcy. In the two years from 1999 to 2001, whilst revenues rose by £700K to almost £2.2m which might look impressive, the overhead would outstrip this and increase by £900K. After 11 straight years of profitability until 2001, this was now the start of 10 years of financial distress and our bottom line changed from showing a net profit of £145K in 1999, to declaring a net loss of £60K in 2001.

The business aphorism *"Turnover is Vanity, Bottom Line is Sanity and Cash is Reality"* is very poignant, since when a business runs out of cash, it goes bust. Our small net loss was nowhere near as bad as our how appalling our cashflow had become, and during this next 12 months, VMI changed from being a cash-positive operation, to one which burned £400K of cash per year. By mid-2001, VMI was fighting for its survival for the first time on my watch.

It started so well when we moved to warm and sunny Kent in May 2000, when the gardens and meadows were bursting into bloom. In case you aren't familiar with the English county of Kent, it is appropriately described as the *Garden of England* and spring is my favourite time of the year.

Our home is situated in the middle of the Weald of Kent, which is a green area of unspoiled beauty which, because of its absence of fast roads and people, we discovered is also a really inconvenient place to live – certainly when you have been used to London! To put this into context, our home is about ten miles from the nearest dual carriageway, five miles from the nearest traffic light and ten miles from the nearest railway station. We live in a holiday region and for much of that first year, we felt that we were taking our first well-earned holiday in the ten years of frenetic working in order to turn my parent's business around.

I wasn't concerned, though, since I believed that I had an effective management structure in place, a solid business and a General Manager to hold things together. Even before I left the cracks started showing but I was assiduously ignoring them, relying instead on my hopeless optimism that everything would be all right, just like Helmslow's exchange in the 1998 film, *Shakespeare in Love*.

"How will it turn out?"

"Strangely enough, it all turns out well."

"How?"

"I don't know, It's a mystery!"

Shakespeare in Love, 1998

The first senior post to depart was my GM, Warren, and though it had taken me three months to find him and six months to train him, Dad couldn't help himself in undermining his authority and he felt that his position had become untenable. Just a few weeks before I was about to move, he left his new Mercedes parked outside the building, put the keys through the letterbox and I never saw him again.

Knowing that Warren would now not hold things together when I left at this critical time, I still had time to change my plans and not move to Kent. This would, once more, see me putting the company before myself, as I had done so many times before. However, this time I was determined to put my family first, though unwisely, I didn't share my fears with Cheryl and doggedly stuck to the plan.

Another of my character flaws at the time, was never to turn back and I am reminded of Marty McFly's experiences in the *Back to the Future* film trilogy, where he could never stand being called

'Chicken'. As a result, when he was inevitably goaded by someone who does call him chicken, he very nearly ruins his entire future before changing his mind and the film has a happy ending. I see now that my stubbornness, resulted in our decision to move to Kent whatever the consequences.

Despite private reservations, we moved and for a time I took a complete back seat with my job and let my management team run the company, relying on the training, systems and procedures that I had implemented. However, I neglected to factor my parents into the plan.

All departments continued to be really busy in early 2000 as the business continued to grow, but in my absence, a state of anarchy had taken hold. The Department heads now treated their divisions more like fiefdoms, jealously protecting them and refusing to operate with one another in order to share equipment, staff and resources, which had previously been our strength.

Management meetings were now very rare and when they did happen, were dysfunctional. Action plans were not followed through and managers not held to account. When the techs couldn't find cameras and radio mics on the shelves to prepare for hires, the operation's manager blamed the crewing department. Instead of resolving the issues, they reserved the missing equipment into a holding order to solve another day but in doing so, reduced the quantity of cameras that we could hire out.

Despite Chau in the accounts department continually yelling that we were spending more buying tape stock consumables than we were generating in sales revenue, no one listened to him. Only much later did I discover that during this time, some £180,000 of cameras, radio mics and tapes were actually being stolen from the company by managers.

Staff left and morale dropped to an all-time low and inevitably, profitability and cash flow plummeted. I had been the glue that had previously held everything together and now that I was gone, the mice gaily played. Oh, and did they play!

Also, our management accounts at this time took some months to prepare and our financial reporting was very basic, so I wasn't to learn the depth of the problems until some months later, during which the situation became ever worse.

Mum would call me up on a daily basis, sobbing on the phone about how terrible things were and I was reminded of the crying telephone calls that we had shared whilst at university. This really stung, since in my mind, she had been the cause of this unpleasant situation but the truth of the matter was that, since I was now the Managing Director, I alone had created the problem, so now I had to fix it.

By Autumn 2000, I resumed going to work once per week, embarking on the grinding five-hour daily commute and soon this turned into two days. Once the full extent of the problem became clear, this became three, four and finally five days per week.

Profitability was to plummet to the worst it had ever been, and this coincided with an increase in lease repayments for a new fleet of vehicles and equipment, which had been specifically purchased for the crewing department, and cash now haemorrhaged from the company.

I persevered with my long daily commutes to stabilise the firm but weak management and loose cost controls meant that, in spite of good revenues, we were about to endure six straight loss-making years as we entered the 2000s.

Discord between the company and Margaret and David, who ran the Crew Division, meant that they decided to leave the company in 2003. Their departure was a major loss to us because they had been the key to retaining the major filming business, and without them, we inevitably lost the Granada Contract and without that, the department was no longer financially viable and resulted in its ultimate closure the following year.

I also fired the Operation's Manager whom I had held responsible for the thefts and losses and whilst things stabilised, revenue continued to decline into the mid-2000s. Saving the company had become my sole focus.

You may be interested to learn that my parents by now had realised their error and together, we did actually try to sell the company. We even instructed a company to represent us to potential buyers. Sadly, this was a forlorn quest, since by now no one was interesting in buying us and these efforts came to nothing.

It was not all bad though, since I left work each day at 3pm, so that I could be home for dinner and experienced all of the milestones of my young son growing up. A funny story happened during this period involving my son and I. I asked a very young Josh what sound a cat made and he replied, "Meow", then likewise a cow and he replied, "Moo". I subsequently pointed to a red chair and asked him, "What colour is it?" and his face broke into a huge smile and he answered proudly, "Blue!" I realised that aged just 15 months, he had little concept of what *cow* and *colour* actually meant, so I now decided to play a game with him, and started teaching him the capitals of the world. We started with England – London; France – Paris and when we ran out of European nations, went on to Asia: Kazakhstan – Astana; Uzbekistan – Tashkent etc. By the end of a few months, he could recite the capitals of more than 100 countries but obviously forgot them as quickly as he had learnt them, though it was fun whilst it lasted!

To ensure that my shorter days were as productive as possible, I was able work on the train using my laptop, and this extended my working day by two-hours. My efforts to make the company more efficient resulted in implementing huge cost-reduction measures to reverse the downward spiral, but however much I tried, profitable trading always seemed to be tantalisingly close but elude us nonetheless.

On a positive note, staff morale improved over time and we achieved the coveted *Investors in People* standard in 2001, reflecting the advances that we had made to being a good employer. The Bassett triumvirate still didn't work well and the stressful and challenging business environment made things harder still.

Our industry was changing very quickly and this was impeding our recovery. As digital equipment had become the norm, our clients were now buying the cheap cameras that we specialised in, rather than always renting them, and our competitors were buying them too. This was to increase competition, reflecting in lower hire rates and resulted in a steadily falling turnover.

I am sure that everyone was regretting not having sold VMI back in 1999 but there was no going back now.

It was time for a new strategy… or going bust.

Chapter 17. A Lie is a Lie is a Lie!

A little inaccuracy sometimes saves tons of explanation.
Saki, "The Square Egg", 1924

I am brutally honest and want to stress that this isn't necessarily the easiest way to live your life but I have made it my own.

A few years ago, I was in my local pub after having played a game of village cricket, when an interesting question was posed. We imagined a situation where our wives tried on a new outfit which they liked but which we felt was not very flattering. The question from our wives was, "Does my bum looked big in this?" and we wanted to know how we might answer this bombshell of a question?

I was really surprised when every one of my team mates responded without hesitation that, in spite of thinking otherwise, they would tell their wives that they thought that the outfit looked lovely! I found this strange and answered that whilst Cheryl has a lovely, slim figure, I thought that she would want to know the truth in such a situation, so of course I *would* tell her so, though perhaps not in such a blunt way.

An apocryphal story also comes to mind of a parishioner who asked his vicar whether a white lie to his mother-in-law was acceptable, if he told her that his lunch had been enjoyable, when clearly it was not. His vicar replied that a lie was a lie, was a lie and that if he had been more honest about his mother-in-law's cooking, then perhaps her cooking would have improved and he would have had an enjoyable lunch!

I agree with him.

Back to 1999, when we had agreed to take over Crystal Television's crewing business, we hadn't actually purchased the going concern of the crewing division. Their company had ceased to trade and we had subsequently employed the staff and freelancers who worked on this production, and invoiced directly to Granada TV. Even though it wasn't in the previous Managing Director's gift to sell us the contract, we had made a handshake deal with him that when VMI took over the contract and previous Crystal TV staff, we would, over time, pay both Margaret, David and himself, a combined £50,000. It had been a handshake deal but this agreement was never formally put into writing.

I had had had every intention of honouring this promise, since it had been made in good faith, though my parents were in no hurry to formalise this arrangement. At first, VMI was suffering from growing pains and later, had other things to think about, such as surviving as a business, so it never became a high priority to formalise this.

We regularly met with Mr Crystal MD and the Margaret/David team, who now ran the VMI crewing division, to discuss how the contract and operation were going. Every time the subject of the written contract and goodwill payment came up, my parents would obfuscate and promise that we would soon finalise this deal and commence paying the agreed sum, just not right now…

Whilst my parents were content with kicking this can down the road, I was not and felt really embarrassed by their conduct. So, when my parents were on holiday during the summer of 2000, I drew up a legal contract committing VMI to pay the £50K over two years to the three of them, in order to formalise our handshake commitment.

Having made several of these agreements in the past, due diligence ensured that what I had written and signed was now legally binding. Consequently, upon returning from their holiday, my parents were *furious* that I had written and signed this contract without consulting them.

We continued to make the agreed goodwill payments over time, in spite of Margaret and David emigrating to the U.S., losing the contract with Granada and VMI going into a financial spiral.

I kept to our word and over the next 2 years, we paid the £50K in full, since I believe that all promises are to be kept.

Chapter 18. I see the future

When fate hands you a lemon, make lemonade. Dale Carnegie

By 2003, I was looking for a new strategy and once again at the annual NAB TV convention in Las Vegas, I was ready to ride the next big innovation wave which would shape the future of TV production.

A little TV history is important here, since big changes were coming. The very first TV design had just 30 vertical lines of resolution and used a really small screen, which is hard to believe now. When the BBC introduced a 405-line standard in 1936, this was originally marketed as High Definition. The next innovation in the early 1970s increased this to 625-lines resolution and was also originally marketed as HD, though we now call it Standard Definition (SD PAL). It was inevitable that the next increment to 1080-lines resolution would be also be called HD and so it was.

By 2003, although VMI had become the main UK rental company specialising in low-end DV-type cameras, we were no longer winning the profitable long hires that we had before, due to a combination of increased competition and also because our clients were now buying these cameras themselves. Since the equipment was also becoming cheaper, I realised that the long-term future of the company was now in jeopardy.

I decided that the strategic direction of the company needed to change to embrace the new HD equipment which seemed to be just on the horizon. This looked to be a perfect fit for us, since the equipment was expensive, which provided good barriers to entry for both our competitors and clients and I had aptitude for the creative flair required to market it.

Sony had introduced their HD format and first HD camera just a few years before but their first model had been large and expensive, with each camera costing more than £70,000, so it was not widely used. You might be interested to learn that George Lucas insisted that Star Wars Episode I was shot with this camera but at the time, this was very rare indeed. Sony recognised the limitations of their earlier camera and had just announced that they planned to release a new HD camera which would be smaller and lighter than the original and might help to make shooting HD more popular too.

While each camera would still cost £50K each, this would be more affordable than the original model, although the accessories to make a shooting kit would still cost another £50K, plus another £50K on top for lenses. I felt though that with some innovative marketing, I could steal a win on all of my competitors who may have bought the original expensive model, and in doing so, reposition VMI as the premier HD rental company in the UK.

Once again, I updated and rewrote my annual business plan (something which I continue to do today) and calculated that as a consequence of our recently run-off leases and improved cost controls, we could immediately afford to invest in £250K of new equipment. This might seem like a brave move since nobody at the time was asking for HD but I believed that in time, viewers would want to watch all programmes in this new format, thus compelling producers to shoot programmes in HD – they just needed a bit of persuading first.

Once again, I wrote a comprehensive marketing plan for presentation to Sony at NAB 2003, and which would include advertising and promotion. It even included booking the Sounds

Nightclub for an all-day event of presentations, and writing a booklet, bravely entitled, 'HD for Producers, all you need to know'. I say bravely, since I first needed to learn the theory.

Sony agreed to my plan and I recall one meeting when we were designing the booklet, which was attended by two Sony executives, who poured over the work that I had done so far. I remember them frowning as they considered some of my word choices, making helpful suggestions for alternative adjectives, such as replacing 'cheap' with 'competitive'. They explained that Sony HD equipment could *never* be described as being cheap!

Having received Sony's blessing, we committed to an initial £250K investment and ordered four of the brand-new Sony HD cameras. The marketing plan went like a dream and once again, over 400 delegates from the TV industry attended our major launch event. When the huge High Definition images were projected for the first time, there was a total hush from the audience, since they had never before experienced such quality. The lack of grain and size of the high-quality images made this an entirely new experience and HD would become an instant success.

I then had a frantic six months visiting all of the top production companies in London to make individual presentations to their most senior producers, and introducing them all to the concepts and arguments of shooting in HD. Each time, I would bring an HD player, HD projector and portable screen with me, as well as my HD reel, so that I could show them large images and make the cogent argument that since they owned the residual rights to their productions, then shooting HD would be in their financial interest too.

I explained that some point in the future, HD would quickly become the norm and when this did happen, any previous programmes mastered in SD would lose all value. I reminded them that since they owned the residual programme rights to their productions, they would quickly be worse off if they continued to shoot today in

Standard Definition (SD). The penny dropped and they immediately switched their production to HD.

Since VMI was one of the few rental companies which stocked this equipment and specifically the new camera model in any quantity, we mopped up. This made an immediate impact to VMI's finances, since HD camera revenue didn't 'crowd-out' any of our existing small camera income. Once again, we were back in the game!

I persuaded the BBC to let me supply HD cameras to shoot a *Holby City* pilot. I visited BBC Elstree to supply HD cameras to allow them to shoot the spoof episode which depicted a surgeon discovering all kinds of extra organs and surgical instruments inside a patient that they had been operating on. They liked the idea of shooting in HD but we were punching too far above our weight at the time, for us to be considered to win a prestigious series like this and we would never supply this series with HD cameras in the future.

I also had my sights set on the BBC's *Dr Who* series, which had recently restarted shooting after a 20-year break but was still being made in SD. I tried so hard to persuade them to switch to HD, explaining about future-proofing the programme but at the time, the producer was simply not interested.

I remember another producer telling me that if HD didn't look like Super-16 film, then flatly, they were not interested. Of course, HD would not look like film, I answered, since it doesn't have the visible grain that S-16 does and instead has a new look, which is filmic, yet high-resolution and clean. This would become the look of the future and whilst they too were not interested in what I had to say at the time, the next 5 years would see all productions switching to HD.

The following 12 months into 2004 would see company revenues rising by an impressive 19 percent, reversing the trend of our recently shrinking revenue, and which was confirmation of the decision to invest in HD. Nonetheless the costs of such a major investment had had a substantially detrimental effect to our finances and we made the largest loss to date for 2004. I didn't mind, as we were again investing in the future.

The author with an early HD Camcorder, circa 2004

Chapter 19. The power of a smile

Believe yourself a failure and that is what you will always be,
however, *know* yourself to be a champion and *that* is what you
will become! Barry Bassett 11/1/13

Travelling on mainline trains during the rush hour takes a bit of
getting used to. Passengers catch the same trains day after day,
travelling on the same carriage and most of them even sit in the
same seat and become cross if they find someone else sitting on it.
The London network is really busy and delays are fairly common, so
any delay quickly raises their stress level. This helps to explain why
people feel pressured when they arrive at their terminus and are
herded through the ticket barriers, greeted by stony-faced train
operatives.

I thought that these train operatives might be miserable as a
consequence of the passengers having a grim disposition
themselves, since I noticed that passengers only rarely smiled at
each other. I had an idea that I might be able to break this cycle, so
I tried an experiment.

For a week, I smiled at the train operatives every time I saw them. I
learned their names, and noticed and complemented them when
they had had a new hair style, and do you know what? They all
began smiling whenever they saw me! This worked with everybody
who worked at Charing Cross station, except one and his name was
Adie.

Adie was a dour ticket collector and he seemed immune to my smile-therapy which did not seem to have any impact on his demeanour. By now, I travelled with a fold-up bicycle, choosing to ride the final part of my journey to work by bike, instead of underground train. This meant that I needed to walk through the manual gate which was often operated by Adie, who made a point of ignoring the passengers and would not take my ticket from me when I walked through the gate. Travelling on a bike, I had no pockets in my cycle jacket and so nowhere to store my ticket and despite trying, Adie continually refused to take my ticket from me. Not a big deal but just a bit irritating for me.

One day, I decided that he WOULD take my ticket, so I stopped walking in the middle of the gate and offered him my ticket. "That's OK", he said, "You have it". "No thank you", I replied. "I have no pockets – please take it from me". This time he lifted up his hands, as if surrendering and actually had a smile – he was enjoying this. "It's fine – you keep it!" I would not back down. "Please take my ticket", I said a little more firmly. By now there was a queue of people behind me, waiting for me to clear the gate, so that they too could get to work but I was not going to back down now, and waited with for his next move with my ticket in my outstretched hand. He was having none of it. "I INSIST, he said – you keep it!" I tried to put in into the breast pocket of his uniform but he went nuts and wriggled like a swarm of ants were inside his shirt, so I deftly placed my ticket onto his shoulder and quickly walked away with him shouting at me. I had won the first round.

A few weeks would pass before I saw Adie again and when I did, I had young Josh with me. We had visited London together and were sat down on a train waiting for it to depart so that we could return home. Out of the corner of my eye, I recognised Adie flanked by 2 policeman walking towards my carriage. I saw them stop outside the window that we were sitting adjacent to, and noticed him pointing at me. The policemen then boarded the train and approached me. At this point, I was really surprised, as this had never happened to me before. They asked me to come with them and I obviously told them no, since the train was about to leave but they informed me that I would not be catching this train. They explained that an allegation had been made against me of an assault charge, which had to be investigated. An assault charge – that's RIDICULOUS!

Anyway, I left the train and after explaining to them what had actually happened a few weeks before, was allowed to catch the next train home with a caution, but I was determined that this incident would not spoil my smiling experiment.

I was to see Adie plenty more times that season and each time that I did, I continued to smile at him and in time, he too began to smile back.

Then one time on my way home, he saw me and unexpectedly grabbed me, and proceeded to hug me, and even told another passenger that I was his BEST FRIEND! We even took a selfie together! It proved that I was right and that a smile had very special properties to make everything and everyone better – and it is free as well!

Barry and Adie in 2011

Chapter 20. Overcooking it

Success is going from failure to failure without losing your enthusiasm. Winston Churchill

Visiting Vegas for the annual NAB TV conference, it is interesting to see the different strategies that gamblers adopt when they play in the casinos. When they are confident that they have a strong hand, seasoned players increase their bets as they believe that the odds are in their favour, and then hold back on their betting when they are less sure.

Business strategy is a bit like this and timing is everything. You want to be the first up the hill but don't want to meet a live dragon when you arrive, else you would have made sure to bring a fireproof suit with you.

In 2003, VMI's HD strategy was going great guns. Revenue was up nearly 20 percent in 2004, in spite of increased competition from another rental company for AVID editing systems. Our competitor's large fleet of AVID systems and deliberately low hire rates meant that it became scarcely profitable for us to compete and we would close this division in 2006. (Hindsight would show us that this competitor's low-pricing strategy would backfire for them too, and they would go bust themselves in a few years' time).

In 2003, VMI had cornered the market for HD camera hire as many of its competitors had bought the earlier, more expensive and heavier HD cameras that their clients no longer wanted, and our marketing was paying off handsomely. We were winning lots of repeat customers too – too many in fact, so my problem became lack of availability, since four cameras simply were not enough to service the amount of work that we were winning.

I was also out two days per week visiting clients in the West End and each time, I would take my HD projector, HD player and screen with me and this was very hard work. My new idea was to build a Soho branch for sales and marketing, incorporating an HD screening room, complete with proper raked cinema seating, allowing me to make regular presentations about the merits of shooting in HD.

I calculated that we could easily afford the costs of running this extravagant facility, with the revenue generated by the additional demand that it would create, and this would allow us to fund increasing our camera fleet from four kits to ten.

We found a building in D'Arblay Street, Soho and rented two floors. We built a reception and office on the ground floor and actually built a 19-seat HD screening theatre in the basement. It was fitted-out with seats ripped out from a Disney screening room and installed with an HD video projector with 3.8m screen, video server and a massive sound system. It looked really smart and much more impressive than our Golders Green building and I remember that it had big wall-to ceiling smoked glass in the reception, too. More practically, we upgraded our telephone system with a new IT infrastructure which would allow us all to work remotely from this new office, and this was a useful precursor to the remote working systems which we would implement in the future too.

Having our own screening room meant that I could now present HD presentations to prospective clients whenever I wanted to. I even managed to persuade Sony's media department which manufactured HD tape stock, to pay for a colour folder for us to give to people with handout notes, which was branded both VMI and Sony Media. I gave my 'HD for Producers' presentation on a regular weekly slot, and usually around a dozen people attended. Many would become clients, so this worked very well.

HD was really taking off in 2004 and we had won so many productions from the BBC and independent producers, that our limited inventory couldn't keep up with orders.

We bought an extra £200K of cameras in early 2004 and then, when strong demand continued, another £500K later that year. For a small company, this was a considerable investment. We could not sustain such high lease payments for all of these cameras at the time, so we worked with a major dealer to purchase this on our behalf and agreed on an extended rent-to-buy arrangement. To make it easier for us, we also agreed a six-month deferral, so that we would not initially pay for these new cameras until the business could sustain it. This was a bit like enjoying a winning streak at cards and then taking all of the winnings and doubling the bet.

It would end badly.

Two things happened which caused the company considerable pain over the next few years. Firstly, in order to make HD equipment more mainstream, both Sony and Panasonic had suddenly reduced their prices by 30 percent, but this only happened after we had paid the higher prices on this large purchase and with expensive funding costs adding to the pain.

I also took my eye of the ball. Since I had moved my office from Golders Green to working full-time in Soho, my attention was no longer on the camera floor and, simply, the quality of our rental service began to suffer. Our clients noticed this but I was blissfully unaware. While I was still successfully winning new business, our camera floor team would let us down. Equipment wasn't well presented, cables would be missing, filters would be scratched and our test facilities were poor. The result was that quite quickly, we stopped winning repeat business and started losing orders to our competitors.

In addition, the spectre of rising costs loomed once more, with the company now servicing both a NW London operation, fully staffed Soho showroom and a separate post production division in West London. Worse still, the company could not easily afford to pay the high lease repayments of the latest purchase tranche, which now looked to be uncompetitively expensive. HD camera equipment was now providing almost a third of annual turnover, so we could not afford to give the equipment back either and uncertainty loomed once more.

Our competitors had caught up with us and were simply doing a better job. It was a really sad time in the company's history, as we struggled to hold on to our clients.

The solution was to increase the quality of our staff and the quality of rental services at the same time as reducing our costs.

This would be a difficult trick to pull off!

Chapter 21. Green shoots

If the highest aim of a captain were to preserve his ship, he would keep it in port forever. Thomas Aquinas

This was a really stressful time for all of us and the relationship between my parents and I became even more fractious than usual. Jay, our most loyal driver who joined VMI in 2005 and is still with us today, recalls that when taking Mum and Dad to Soho to attend a meeting with me, he would ask Dad in a playful way to make sure that he behaved nicely! Dad would sometimes call him just a short time later, after he had exploded with anger at me and ask Jay to collect him again.

On the 8 November 2006, we faced such a severe cash flow crisis, that once again we found ourselves on the brink of insolvency and urgent, decisive action was again required.

Annual revenues had dropped to pre-2000 levels and there was now no possibility that we could afford to pay the really expensive leases which had been previously agreed, and we were already £57K in arrears. Although it seemed that I had always been looking at cost-saving measures for the company, I now needed to attack costs even more savagely and to do this fast, or else we could expect a visit from the bailiffs, who would impound our equipment and we would close for good.

In order to survive, I estimated that we had to cut 20 percent from our costs any way that we could. We returned whatever cars we could to the leasing companies, sold any equipment that we felt that we could do without and shed whatever staff we felt that were not essential for the business as it was now.

Mum and I refinanced all of our leasing agreements, including the heavy deferred lease agreement, to ensure that our cashflow break-even was at a much more realistic level that the business could sustain – But this wasn't enough, so all three Directors were forced to take substantial pay cuts in order to balance the books. Since my parent's combined income was much more than I earned at the time, Cheryl and I really suffered - though more on this later.

About this time, BBC Radio 4 ran a weekly radio programme, where they would interview clever people in difficult industries, like climatology, and ask them challenging questions which they knew couldn't easily be answered, such as, why can't they can't predict the weather a year ahead...? The programme was called 'If you are so clever, why aren't you rich?' and I kept wondering to myself, how a clever guy like me could have got it so very wrong.

It was clear to me by now that we didn't have the right skills to run a cine-camera rental company. We had entered this industry from the low-end wedding sector, and our clients now shot commercials and film productions and expected a higher level of service from us than we were used to providing. With rare exception, our technicians didn't have the right backgrounds either, so we needed to bring in some new expertise.

In June 2006, Kevin joined VMI. He had had the perfect film background lacking in all of us, and had previously worked in, and trained at, the best companies in our industry. He joined us after his previous company had gone bust and where he had held the position of Technical Director. Interestingly, this was the same company that had offered to buy us seven years before.

Kevin recalls that he had been asked to attend six separate interviews with Dad, but he wasn't convinced that we needed him. Surprisingly, some months later Dad *still* didn't think that Kevin was right for the company, and we used to have many arguments about this. He would shake his head disparagingly and utter that, "Kevin just isn't right, you know…" It made me really cross too, since I realised that Kevin had such valuable expertise and we needed his help extremely badly.

To begin with, since Kevin worked out of Golders Green and I, out of Soho, we didn't work together or even meet for some time. Kevin recalls not even being aware that I was particularly important to the company, and just thought that I was the son of the founders who perhaps, 'played' in Soho, as a sort of vocation!

Kevin had some really good ideas of how he could improve our service, and some of these were at little or no cost to us, such as helping with training which would increase the standards of prep and knowledge. Others, though, were expensive, like replacing all of our flight cases. Mum made it really clear to him, that there was literally no money available for initiatives, so he did what he could with a very limited budget.

The truth was that VMI was flat broke. After six struggling years, my parents were not receptive to spending money, in order to increase the standards of our service but I was, and slowly we made progress and our clients noticed it.

Steadily, business improved and whilst VMI was to post the sixth annual loss in a row, we could finally see a way out of our predicament for the first time in a very long while.

By the end of 2006, revenue was up and our clients were happier. Staff morale had improved too, costs were under control and our cashflow was positive for the first time in some years.

VMI was finally on the road to recovery.

Then in December 2006, VMI suffered its worst burglary of all time and we would later find out that we were also not insured.

Chapter 22. Working from home

The reasonable man moulds himself around the world, whereas the unreasonable man moulds the world around himself. Therefore, all of humanity's progress relies on the unreasonable man. George Bernhard Shaw.

These days I work from home four days per week aided by an excellent fibre optic internet connection and dedicated hardware but it hasn't always been like this. To begin with, people thought me mad even for trying.

It had always been a plan of mine that when we moved to Kent, I would part work mostly from home but back in 2000, forget about fibre, broadband, or ADSL to connect to the internet, we had to use dialup, and this meant making a phone call just to connect to the internet. Of course, it also meant that I needed to make another phone call if I wanted to speak to anyone in the office as well, so working from home was both unproductive, frustrating and *hard*. I persevered, as I wanted it to improve and didn't give up until I was happy.

VMI's first computer system was called AVAIL and it was a text-based system which gave the impression that it belonged to the 1980s, but it was fast and the small packets of data that it used meant that it could work effectively over a dialup connection. I experimented connecting to the server with a Blackberry mobile phone and remember being very impressed when it worked. I would often connect to it remotely to continue working on the train home.

My first business lines at home used ISDN-2 which incorporated two separate business telephones lines in one cable. I would usually make two simultaneous phone calls when I was working, so that one enabled my computer to interface with the server at work and the other for me to call the warehouse or the rental desk. Of course, I would also need a third phone line to speak to clients as well and whilst it sort-of worked, it was very slow and unsophisticated.

However, with the development of the new IT infrastructure in Soho, and the arrival of broadband to Kent at about the same time in 2003, working from home became much more practical. For the first time, I was able to configure an extension of my phone system to be at home, and avoiding diverting calls to my mobile, which made it so much easier than before. A single button on my extension handset allowed me to choose either to receive calls either at my phone extension at home or in Soho.

My old university friend, Mike, had become an IT specialist by this time, and we experimented together to refine our system, since it was not perfect and periodically, my calls would prematurely cut off mid-conversation and the phone would go dead, which was very frustrating.

We continued to play with floating IP addresses and then fixed IP addresses and then dedicated hardware VPNs, and each small refinement would make a small but noticeable improvement. Then a new phone system and better internet allowed me to remotely log into my actual phone extension and route my calls in a more sophisticated way than I could do before, and as the internet improved, so did my productivity and the reliability of the system.

Today, all who work at VMI's Bristol branch are effectively remote workers, and I have set up home working stations for all of the Directors and Managers, to help them to achieve a better work/life balance.

Some years ago, I had the idea of building an active desk. Some people use a treadmill but I like bicycles, so my first version included a recumbent bike which I fitted under my desk at home but the seat was *really* uncomfortable. I even built one of these setups in the office in London, so that the Rental Desk could take it in turns to use it and enable them to work and ride for short bursts. Few were as keen as I to sit on a bike, so it wasn't used very much.

Today, I have a full-sized stationary bike at my desk and will work and ride for 90 minutes at a time on an average day and do this, four days per week. People say how great it is for me to work from home and I agree with them – it *is* great but they perhaps don't realise just how long it took, before it all worked properly.

I've found that if you really want something to work which is a bit different to the norm, then persevere – it will be worth it in the end.

PART IV

Chapter 23. 16 December 2006. Burglary

Reality is harsh. It can be cruel and ugly. Yet no matter how much we grieve over our environment and circumstances nothing will change. What is important is not to be defeated, to forge ahead bravely. If we do this, a path will open before us. Daisaku Ikeda

In mathematical chaos theory, the butterfly effect describes circumstances where a small change in initial conditions, such as the fluttering of a butterfly's wings in Osaka, Japan, might cause a really big change elsewhere, like a hurricane in Florida.

It seemed a fitting metaphor to use my beloved mathematical chaos theory to show that that the actions of the Crew department staff some three years before, would now result in the worst fight of my life.

We were good employers and genuinely cared about the people who worked for us. Of course, between my parents and I, we often argued on how to best to achieve this, but attention to security was certainly an area where we all did agree.

Back in 2003 when we had integrated the crewing department to move into our main building, the unpredictable demands of filming news, meant that people now worked around the clock, so we had implemented measures to protect both the staff and the equipment.

We fitted panic buttons around the building and these would alert the police to a possible burglary without the alarms wailing. These small boxes were the size of cigarette packets and carefully designed so that they could not be triggered by accident.

Around this time, the latest anti-theft innovation was the 'Smoke Cloak', which, once triggered by an alarm activation, would quickly fill the space with opaque smoke and disorientate any would-be burglars, thus limiting what they were able to steal. A policeman had told me that they were so effective, that when the police arrived at a recent break-in call-out, some burglars were actually still inside the building, entirely lost and disorientated by the smoke. We all agreed that we needed a Smoke Cloak, so we instructed our alarm company to install one in the equipment area, which they did, terminating it with a 13A plug where we would later find out the cleaner did the vacuuming. More on this later.

On a random day in early 2004, a crew coordinator idly wondered what might happen if he pressed both of the buttons on the strange device which had been installed under his desk. Sure enough, some minutes later, having activated the new panic button system, a police car arrived and realising that this was a false alarm, they left.

What was important about this specific event was that it was the third such false alarm in six months, and under the terms of our agreement, the police would now impose a penalty of withholding their remote monitoring service to us for three full months. This was a blow, since without police monitoring, we also no longer satisfied the terms of our insurance. For this three monthly period, we were doubly careful with security, knowing that for this temporary time we were not insured and waited eagerly for it to pass.

On the day that marked the end of the three-month period, since we were not permitted to liaise with the police directly, Mum telephoned the alarm company and requested that they restore the police monitoring service immediately. To remind you, this was the very same alarm company who had previously fitted the panic buttons and the smoke cloak and now were responsible for restoring our police monitoring service.

During that fateful phone call, the alarm company confirmed that they would restore this service but unwisely, Mum had not decided to put this request in writing, either with a fax, letter or email – just a phone call...

Then three years later on the 16 December 2006 at 2am, a gang of thieves, broke into the main building and carried out an audacious burglary.

The smoke cloak would have really slowed them down and prevented much from being stolen but the cleaner had not plugged the device back into the power socket when he had completed the vacuuming. Without power, it was useless.

The police should have come quickly too and the sound of their sirens would have forced the burglars to hurry up and leave early, but with no active monitoring system in place, they did not come either.

So, instead of a smash and grab, these thieves took their time and made off with an enormous haul of cameras, lenses and other specialist equipment, which we would later value at around £600,000.

What made this even worse, was that that we had just taken delivery of two of the very latest top-of-the-range Sony HD cameras, which had been bought specifically to supply a production who ought to have been shooting a feature film that week. My frustration was that the client had changed their minds at the last minute and instead of hiring them from us, had now hired them from a competitor. So as well as losing the production hire revenue, we now also lost a further £104,000 worth of cameras too, which were still unopened in their original cardboard cartons.

§

Chapter 24. The aftermath

Two things are infinite: the universe and human stupidity; and I'm not sure about the universe. Albert Einstein

Whilst this robbery was really annoying and inconvenient, we were confident of being fully covered by our insurance policy, so we cleaned up the mess and made a full stocktake of what was missing, after which we submitted a hefty insurance claim to our insurance company.

The robbery happened less than a week before we were due to break up for our fortnight Christmas holiday and to our shock and dismay, we had just been informed that our police monitoring service was not active. We made a formal request to our alarm company to reinstate the service but they were adamant that this would take 21 working days to go live, so, with no other options available and not wanting to risk being uninsured again, we hired a security firm to supply a 24-hour security guard with dog to patrol our buildings over the entire Christmas break and until the monitoring service was resumed in January.

There is always a delay of some months between making an insurance claim and receiving a pay-out, and being a major claim, the insurance company had assigned a claim's investigator to us, who started work in earnest in early January 2007.

We had already completed a major cost-cutting exercise just a few months previously, and now made the reasonable assumption that our business interruption insurance policy would pay for whatever additional costs we faced as a consequence of the burglary.

We had lost a lot of equipment in this loss. Much of it belonging to the finance companies but the leases still needed to be paid and until these cameras were replaced, our reduced stock had a hugely detrimental effect on our ability to earn revenue.

We hired-in replacement equipment from other companies when we were short, because our equipment had been stolen and bought new cameras when they were needed for long jobs. All suppliers were told that they would have to wait for payment until the insurance pay-out was made.

Seeing that we were very concerned about the uncertainty of the claim, the insurance investigator had told us not to worry, since if we could prove that we had been paying for the police monitoring service, then *of course* we would be covered. We obligingly provided invoices which we had paid over the past three years to confirm this, but on doing so, the insurance company did not immediately offer us the reassurance that we had been expecting. Instead, the investigation continued into February, March and April and as time passed, we began to become more and more concerned as our bills mounted alarmingly.

We were still puzzled as to why the police claimed that we didn't have the police monitoring service in place at the time of the burglary, since Mum definitely had phoned them to request this. Over time though, we realised that the alarm company must not have actioned her verbal request in that fateful call, three-years before.

On contacting the alarm company, they informed us that they had a record of a phone call which had taken place on the day in question with my Mum but no detailed notes existed about exactly what was discussed. It didn't matter that this call had occurred exactly three months from the date that the monitoring service had been withdrawn – it was obvious what the subject would have been about, and what we would have asked them to do, but they would not be drawn into this.

I cannot stress how hard these months were and everybody became very dejected as we began to face the possibility that the insurance company might wriggle out of paying us at all. In which case, our debts would almost certainly wipe us out.

As a rule, I don't give up, but the future seemed so uncertain now. I started exploring the unthinkable and even applied for some jobs. These came to nothing but reminds me that I really was now at rock bottom.

Chapter 25. Be careful what you aim for

Watch your thoughts, for they become words. Watch your words, for they become actions. Watch your actions, for they become...habits. Watch your habits, for they become your character. And watch your character, for it becomes your destiny! What we think we become. My father always said that, and I think I am fine. Margaret Thatcher, as portrayed in the film 'The Iron Lady'.

When I was studying my MBA, I remember being told of a study where a group of Harvard undergraduates were interviewed before they graduated and asked about their five year plan. A follow-up study looked at what they were doing five years later and most importantly (remember this is a U.S. study), how much they earned. What was fascinating was that there was a 100 percent correlation between those who had had a plan earning more money in time than their peers. What their plan was and whether they had achieved it was not a factor here, only that they had had a plan.

I love the above quote and have said it so many times to my son that he can recite it without thinking. To me, this is a really poignant quote because I have planned my entire life and at this stage, I don't mind admitting, that it hadn't gone very well.

In life, it is crucial to aim for achieving the balance of planning for the future and also enjoying the here and now, though this, of course is an ideal.   At times, you don't have this luxury and simply have to do what needs to be done in order to survive. The burglary and its aftermath didn't stop me from planning, nor aiming to improve my life balance but that would have to wait for now.

I value loyalty, hard work, honesty, integrity, intelligence as well as kindness but above all, I feel that the character trait that I value most in myself is determination.

In my twenties, I wanted to be a wealthy man and then this became a dutiful son and today, a better person.

These days however, I now measure my income by my laughter lines, *not* my bank account. My wife tells me that on this measure, I am wealthy indeed!

Chapter 26. The uninsured Loss

It's not whether you get kicked down on the floor – what counts is whether you get back up again. Anon

Late in the afternoon of Monday 4 June, Mum asks me into Dad's office, which in itself was rare.

They were both standing motionless with grim, steely expressions on their faces trying hard not to betray the boiling turmoil that they were feeling inside.

"They aren't going to honour the claim," she said calmly.

That was it – just seven words and our hopes of a happy outcome crumpled.

"I just spoke to them on the phone and they told me straight. The Directors had a personal responsibility to ensure that we had police monitoring service in place and as we clearly didn't, they are not going to honour the claim citing breach of terms."

"They are going to hide behind this technicality and wriggle out of paying."

"That's it – no appeal?" I ask vainly.

"That's it."

"Can we sue the alarm company?"

"No chance. Their terms and conditions are pretty air-tight to protect them from third party liability."

"What is the actual financial position as of today?" I ask.

"Well, we owe our suppliers £339K, VAT
of £79K, £29K of PAYE and we also owe
the factoring company £120K," said
Mum.

"So, we actually owe almost £600K?
Wow," I said glumly.
"How much is in the bank?"

"Actually, we have literally no money."

"Can it be any worse?" I asked
"Since the financial restructure of last
year, we have not been able to keep up
with the lease repayments either and are
now £15,000 in arrears, so we are now
in danger of having our cameras
repossessed."

"It gets worse!
…and the insurance company definitely
said that they wouldn't honour the
claim? We were relying on that
£600K."

"No. They told me definitively today that
this was their final decision."

"BASTARDS! They could have told us
this six months ago so that we could
have cut our costs further instead of
waiting for a pay-out that they had no
intention of honouring."
"And now it is just too late…"
"We owe almost £600K which works
out at about five months of revenue; we
have very little equipment that wasn't
stolen which we can rent out and

actually earn us revenue; we owe £15K in overdue leases and you are telling me that we have *no money*?" I said

"...and don't forget the £250K of personal guarantees that we have to the leasing companies if we go bust," said Dad.

The three members of the VMI board all looked at each other grimly. Business failure looked certain.

"Right then, I am going to have to think of a plan," I said.

This was met by silence.

"I'm off for a bike ride. Geneva to Cannes through the Alps should do it. 1000km and 21 Alps. See you in two weeks and I WILL have a plan".

Chapter 27. An awful choice

The definition of insanity is doing the same thing over and over again and expecting a different outcome. Albert Einstein

A famous thought experiment of mathematical Game Theory creates a scenario where a train is hurtling out of control and in about 20 seconds, will smash into a station where it will kill hundreds of people. You alone are next to the controls where you can avoid this from happening by remotely change the track points to divert the train but to your horror, you can see a child who is playing on the alternative track and who will be killed if you take this action.

It is just a thought experiment but researchers have found that no one wants to make an active choice which will directly cause the avoidable death of a single individual, even if this action can avoid several other deaths.

I find that if you don't like something and find yourself in a difficult situation, then you have three choices.

    i)   Do nothing
    ii) Do something about it.
    iii) Sit on it and wait – oh no, this is actually the same as i)…

I could now see now that the money that we owed was approaching the value of the entire company's assets including the valuable freehold, so we were close to being insolvent and trading illegally.

Kevin had a film background and had been brought in to help the company improve its rental standards but had not been given either a free hand nor the money to achieve this. A partnership with Kevin and I running the firm now seemed to offer the company the best chances of recovery and restoring it to profitability, but there was an enormous barrier to overcome first before we could do this. Dad had to agree to leave his company and if he didn't, then I would need to force him out or face the consequences.

The choices available to me now were bleak.

1. I could keep things as they were and clearly, without changing the very basics of the business, we would go bust. I would lose everything but would keep the relationship with my parents. I didn't like this one.

2. My parents could leave the company (either voluntarily, or not…) and then Kevin and I could completely reinvent it and turn it into a great success. This was a huge challenge given the depth of the financial mess that we were now in and was unlikely to succeed anyway. Besides which, my relationship with my parents and in particularly with Dad, would suffer too. However, if we *did* succeed, then it would protect my parents from suffering financial hardship and they would keep the value of their shares. I didn't really like this one either.

3. The Nuclear option. I did actually have a third choice and several of my friends urged me to consider it. By voluntarily liquidating the company and buying back all of the assets at a great discount, then all of our suppliers' debts would be wiped clean and with lower financial commitments, we would have the best chances of success. However, Kevin and I would now own 100 percent of the new shares outright and my parents would end up with nothing. This would be my best personal outcome for sure but would also destroy my relationship with my parents without any hope of a reconciliation – but could I do this to my parents?

143

I was about to go for the longest cycle ride in my life and which would give me two full weeks to think. It weighed heavily on my mind but however much I thought about it, I knew that I could not bring myself to burn my parents.

Chapter 28. Cycling

Rules are for the obedience of fools and the guidance of wise men. Douglas Bader

I used to ride a bicycle when I was at school but after I bought my first car then just like my friends, I never looked back.

After we moved to Kent, I was to discover that exercise was really difficult to fit into a commuting lifestyle, since I would leave home early in the morning and by the evening, was simply too tired and the prospect of taking a car journey just to keep fit, became too much effort for me.

I tried many different sports over the years, some of which I still keep up but in late 2006, I tried a new strategy and decided to take up cycling again.

I realised that since the closest railway station to my home was ten miles away, up and down the rolling hills of Kent, so riding to the station would itself be a workout and returning home again would be another workout too. I was going to make the trip to the station in any case, so it shouldn't even eat much into my day either, I thought, though when I first tried this journey, I don't mind confessing that it half-killed me.

However, I persevered riding an old steel-framed trail bike, initially cycling two days per week and then occasionally three days per week with a rest day in between.

It was about this time that I was approached to sponsor a charity media bike ride through the Alps called *The Fireflies* which was a group that had started in 2000 to raise money for Leukaemia research and continues to ride today. https://thefirefliestour.com/.

I lent them a video camera so they could shoot a film of the 2006 ride and which would help to raise awareness for their cause, and I was invited to the film screening later that year. I remember watching a piece-to-camera by a Fireflies cyclist, who gave his account of the long, arduous climb up the Col de la Madeleine. This is an exhausting 25km climb to the summit (Col) and mid-way, he explained how he had rung his friend to tell him how much he was suffering but instead of sympathising, his friend reminded him that when he eventually got off his bike, his pain would stop but for those with Leukaemia, their pain would continue. He commanded him to, "Endure the Pain!"

This really inspired me and I spontaneously decided that I too would become a Firefly rider and raise £10,000 for their cause by riding the Alps in June of 2007. It didn't matter that my life and business were inherently uncertain, training for the Alpine Fireflies ride provided a welcome distraction for me, so I bought a road bike and began training.

About this time, the rules governing travelling on trains with full-sized bicycles had changed, and now during peak-time journeys, you could only carry fold-up bikes. I had secured special permission from the Charing Cross Station Manager to allow me to travel on these busy trains during the spring and summer of 2007 with a full-sized road bike, so I trained and in time, my three days riding to the station became four days and then five days per week.

I did lots of training rides at the weekends too, concentrating on riding hills and becoming used to being in the saddle for five hours or more at a time. All veteran *Fireflies* had told me that there weren't any hills in the UK that could properly prepare you for cycling over

21 alpine mountains, since these mountains were BIG and cycling 1000km for eight days with just one rest day was *hard,* and they were right. However, by the time that the summer was approaching, my wife recalls that my thighs looked like muscular chicken legs which were totally out of proportion with the rest of my body!

I continued riding to the station and by September of that year, I realised that I had not filled my car with fuel since April and made the brave (some say stupid) decision to sell it. I knew that this would commit me to riding to the station from that point on, even in sideways hailstones and torrential rain.

The Scandinavians have an aphorism that there is no such thing as bad weather, only bad clothing and I can attest to this with my now-extensive cycle wardrobe. I sold my car in late 2007 and we have been a single car family ever since. When I work in London, I continue to ride my bike to the station, even in snow and driving rain.

The Fireflies send-off event was on the 8 June, when I met the other riders for the first time. Filled with trepidation, I travelled to Lake Geneva on 10 June and from my hotel room, I could see the majestic peaks across the expanse of water that I would soon be cycling over. The following morning of the 11 June 2007, 50 riders started the eight-day ride to cross 1000km and 21 Alps by bicycle.

During the weeks before, I'd managed to raise £6,500, mainly by asking individuals to donate and this seemed to be even more effort than the training and the riding.

The ride however was exhilarating and gave me many hours to consider my predicament, and the break provided a welcome opportunity for me to really think about the life journey that I had taken and where my future might lay.

I thought about how I had originally only joined the company in order to assist my parents, because Mum had implored me to, and remembered that she had even been prepared for me to forego my degree to do this.

Then I had put all of my life plans on hold whilst I tried to help them and had never received any thanks for it.

In my early to mid-20s, when I had few responsibilities and could have easily left to start my career, we all pulled in different directions but I continued to put my needs after those of my parents' and loyally remained with the company.

Then again in my late twenties when I made the decision to forge a career for myself in the city, once again, Mum engineered the situation which enforced me to stay against my wishes. Later when I achieved my aim of finding a buyer for the company, then again Mum was responsible for preventing me from leaving.

My excellent plan to move to Kent had also backfired, as Mum and Dad had sabotaged this from working properly, resulting in my General Manager quitting and allowing the mismanagement of the company in my absence.

When Josh came of school age, we later found that our local school was oversubscribed and had been obliged to send him to a private prep school. To begin with we didn't mind, since I was initially well paid, but as the school fees ramped up and which coincided with me taking several substantial pay cuts, we really suffered financially.

Unlike me, Josh developed to be very creative and eventually went on to study graphic design at university, rather than taking the academic route. This meant that the grammar school system that we had planned for him now no longer suited, so we were now obliged to remain with the private school system after all, and faced eight more years of school fees.

My parents knew that we had reduced our mortgage payments to interest-only and were actually partly drawing-down on our mortgage for some years, just to top up my salary, so that we could live. They were aware too that we also had personal guarantees on our house, but this didn't seem to concern them.

Finally, by not putting the request to reinstate the police monitoring service in writing, Mum had directly caused the latest crisis.

I was now 39 with little chance of a second career and the truth was that with a mortgage, family and private school fees, I was now trapped and needed this job.

However, I remembered the lesson that I had learned on the first day of my MBA when the paper tower couldn't be built, because of multiple Major Generals. The three Bassetts were all Major Generals pulling in different directions. Our metaphoric tower would never be built if we remained together.

I recognised how important Kevin was for the company's recovery but only I seemed to be the one who fully realised his value.

After many years of trying to support my parents in a secondary role, my conclusion was that if VMI were to be saved, then I would need to take full control and in doing so, this would safeguard everyone's financial future.

The company needed me in order to survive, so I would need to make the next move.

Two weeks later, I returned to London with reality waiting for me.

The author at the top of the Col De La Madeleine Climb, 2007

Chapter 29. Crunch time

The hardest lessons in life to learn are which bridges to cross and which to burn. Frederick Hesburgh

The morning of Monday 25 June arrived and I entered the kitchen dressed as usual in my cycle gear, since of course, I now cycled to the station every day. This morning I was to attend a crucial board meeting to decide on the future of the company and this would be attended by our accountant and I could not be late.

I usually allowed 35 minutes to cycle the hilly 14km (10m) ride to the station and had only broken 30 minutes once before and had an irritating habit of cutting this fine. However just before leaving, I glanced at my watch and realised in horror that the microwave clock was running five minutes fast. I did a mental calculation that the train would actually depart in 29 minutes, so I grabbed my bike and rode like I had never ridden before and 27 mins 55 seconds later, I boarded the train to London. I have never equalled this time since that day.

Ninety minutes later I arrived at the office, changed and entered the meeting room. During my journey, I had run through all of the options over and over again in my head, and now I knew exactly what I had to do.

Both of my parents were waiting for me and the short wait before the accountant arrived was tense. All three of us were pensive and whilst the experience of riding a bike through the Alps had given me a lot that I could have talked about, I found that even I couldn't speak much.

Eventually, both Kevin and Nick entered the room. Nick had been our accountant for several years and had now become both a friend, advisor and when required, a mediator to stop the Bassetts from fighting. I had invited Kevin to attend. He was central to my plan and we had spoken at length over the weekend.

I opened the meeting and gave a precis of the situation.

"Our creditors have been eagerly waiting for our insurance pay-out and now that it is not coming, they won't wait any longer."

I continued, "With what we owe the main equipment dealer and the other creditors including VAT, other taxes, factoring and lease arrears, it is absolutely clear now that we cannot survive. Without immediate and decisive action, we are facing certain bankruptcy."

This was not new information but as I uttered these words, they seemed to take on a new meaning, like having a judge committing me to a life jail sentence.

I looked at my parents now: "Whilst you and Mum have assets, I only have my home and a large mortgage. The personal guarantees which are certain to be activated should we go pop, will mean that I will lose everything and I am not prepared for this to happen without a fight."

There was silence as I delivered this and nobody said anything. I began to perspire and could feel my heart thumping beneath my shirt.

"We owe £578,000 and any one of the companies that we owe money to, can *at any time* issue us a wind-up petition which will close us down and then that will be it. Doors closed. We simply *have* to show them that we are a *new* board with *new* ideas, so that they will have the confidence to support us."

There was still a deathly silence from everyone in the room, except the sound of my voice and I felt a deep sense of unease at what I was now about to say. I was sure that the sound of my racing heart was audible to the others in the room, as it sounded really loud to me.

"We have only two options," I said.

I had already decided that I wasn't going to burn my parents and didn't even think that it would help the situation to mention the nuclear option, even just in passing.

"Either we go bust and lose everything and this for me is not an option, or…"

I was still their dutiful son but I was also a survivor and I knew what was coming.

"I consider that the best chance for our survival is for Kevin and I to work together in partnership, where I run sales, marketing and finance, leaving Kevin, with his excellent technical skills, to run the camera floor. We plan to reposition VMI from where it is, as an 'also-ran' camera hire company, to one known for its excellent service. This will be very hard to achieve but it is the best chance that we have to save the company from certain ruin."

My parents did not move their attention from looking at me. Mum already knew what I was going to say and had agreed to go along with the plan but I hadn't spoken to Dad since returning from France, as I knew that this would not go down well with him. His face still maintained a grim, funereal expression and though I looked carefully, his face betrayed little else.

I continued to look at my parents, pausing momentarily for impact: "…so, Kevin and I should become sole Directors and the two of you should voluntarily agree to leave the board.", I said.

153

I then waited a while for this to fully sink in and looked at my Dad now with imploring eyes: "If you and Mum don't resign, then our creditors simply won't trust us to change course and they will close us down and we will all lose *everything*."

I did not waver in my intensity: "But the upside from your position is that you will both keep the majority of your shareholding and over time, will also lose your Personal Guarantees as well."

I thought that this was a generous offer – after all, I was taking all of the risk and Kevin and I would be doing all of the work. They would still retain their shareholding too. Dad's face remained tight. I could guess what he was thinking and I would much rather be elsewhere right now and the worst was still to come.

I glanced at Mum and it was clear that she was ready to say out loud what I wanted to hear.

"I agree to resign as a Director," she said.

I nodded appreciatively.

I looked at Dad. His face had darkened but he still said nothing. I could see that he was furious but was working hard to keep a lid on it.

The silence was deafening and as we all looked at each other, our eyes flicked from one person to another, we tried to make some sense from the unfolding situation.

It was very clear that we were all waiting for Dad to respond to this and eventually, he said angrily, "You can't do this - I have rights, you know!"

His head was now shaking slightly and I had been here, many times before. This meant that he was boiling inside and about to explode. I could see that he was clearly very angry but at least he wasn't shouting yet, I thought. That would come later.

I kept my voice impassive, as I wasn't going to fuel a shouting match: "Dad, you don't have automatic rights to remain a Director," I said calmly. "Mum and I control 65 percent of the shares, so if you don't resign then I will have no option but to force you out. This is the law."

He continued to stare at me and his face was now shaking visibly.

"Please don't make me do this," I said quietly.

"You have to do what you have to do," he said and then left the room.

We all looked at each other in amazement – it wasn't supposed to have gone like this.

I went into Dad's office and spent the next 90 minutes trying to explain my reasoning to him and the ramifications of doing nothing but he was unyielding and uncompromising. He would NOT go.

His volume rose and rose until eventually his shouting could be heard throughout the entire building. He yelled that if forced out, then he would set fire to the entire building. He would rather do this, than give it to me. He kept yelling to me that I was not his equal! All I wanted to do was to save the company and my own skin but he was having none of it.

It was really sad to hear him say these words and it was clear that he felt betrayed by me and I began to have some doubts that I was doing the right thing after all. I stayed strong and held my nerve.

Nick then spent the next two hours also trying to reason with him but Dad clearly felt that the time for being reasonable had passed. This was a direct attack on him if war is declared, then in his book you *never* surrender.

We reconvened in the meeting room once he had calmed down a bit but his face still had the same bitter, grim expression of before. I knew then that he would never forgive me for what I was about to do but just like his position 12 years before, I felt that I had no other option.

The rest of the meeting was a formality.

I put forward a motion to make Kevin a Director, since companies need to have at least two Directors by law and Mum and I voted this through.

Then, with my heart in my mouth, I put forward a motion to vote Dad out from the company that he had set up, that he loved and that gave him an identity.

There was again silence as Mum and I formally voted him out.

He looked at me with cold hateful eyes. It was done.

This was the hardest decision that I had ever taken and now would come the hardest period in my life too.

I needed to deliver and to save VMI, otherwise it would have all been for nothing.

PART V

Chapter 30. The slow recovery

To achieve great things, two things are needed: a plan and not quite enough time. Leonard Bernstein

A joke states that running a company, you only have to work half-days. Simple - you choose which twelve hours!

Kevin and I meant business. We started as we meant to go on, fighting on all fronts and working at least twelve-hour days to begin with.

I could never have achieved the company's recovery without Kevin's help and we both worked tirelessly together with the shared common goal of us surviving the first three months. When the first three months had passed and we were still in business, we extended our goal to survive for another three months; and when that period arrived and we were still trading, we set ourselves a more ambitious goal of surviving for the next six months. We didn't really rest until 2012 and always felt that we were living on borrowed time.

We both had a very long what-to-do list and started work immediately.

The first task was to draw up an action plan to manage the company's debts. Since any of our creditors could at the time have submitted a wind-up petition to close us down, it became essential that we adopted a complete change of approach and we were proactive in engaging both our staff, our clients and our creditors.

We consulted with an organisation who had promised to park all of our debts into an arrangement called a CVA (Compulsory Voluntary Arrangement). This would protect us from any attempts to shut us down by issuing us with a wind-up petition. After a week of them working, during which they had entered all creditors' invoices into their system and were ready to press the button to commence repayment negotiations, did we hit a snag.

We suddenly realised that in this type of financial arrangement, we were forbidden from buying any more equipment on finance, until we had paid off *every* creditor. Not being able to sign leases to buy the latest kit would be immensely limiting to our recovery, so having realised that the CVA idea was a mistake, we now cancelled our agreement with them but before this could be done, we had to part with £6,000 of hard-earned and very valuable cash. Arghh!

I now worked on a three-year business plan which would see us paying off all debts and presenting this to all of our creditors for approval. I speedily wrote this and personally agreed unofficial repayment plans with everyone, and so began our new partnership and 3 years of very hard work to restore the firm to profitability.

I had dinner one evening with Peter Zac, who ran our West London edit facility, and negotiated an agreement, where he and his partner would buy the edit business outright from us for £100K. I was extremely pleased with this result, but on telling Mum my good news, instead of her being happy, she criticised me for selling it too cheaply! Now *I knew* that I had made the right decision to go it alone. We had closed our AVID rental division the previous year, and this would spell the end of VMI having any editing or post production facilities, relying solely on rental revenue to power the business going forward.

It was also essential for us to give up our Soho facility too, since this was both really expensive to run and also deemed non-essential. The lease remained our responsibility, so I advertised the two floors of the D'Arblay Street building to sublet it, and found two guys, Claudio and Hennan, who wanted to turn this into a café. The best news was that they wanted to continue working with us to run the downstairs screening room, and for it to retain our branding. The deal agreed was that I would provide and look after the equipment and they would pay the bills – result!

They branded it the 16mm Café, and it would soon become a regular place for me to meet clients in Soho and avoid the enormous overhead. We became good friends and Hennan taught me how to make quiche and shortcrust pastry. Sadly, the high cost of rent and business rates would mean that this too would close down in two years' time, since even they struggled to pay the bills and make a profit.

Once again, old assets were ruthlessly sold and we worked hard to stick to the repayment plans that we had promised. Over time, VMI's historic debts (for suppliers, taxes and overdue leases) reduced from £429K in April 07 to £200K in April 08 to £65K in May 2010 and finally nil in 2011. We made sure that everybody was paid every penny that we owed.

However, the video dealer that we had owed £169K to back in 2007, what of them? We made sure that they were paid everything that we owed them too, although it would take us three years to achieve this. They were very impatient and extremely unpleasant to deal with, and during this time, issued us with three separate wind-up petitions and we had to fight them all. Their justification was that we had not paid them back quickly enough, but we demonstrated to the courts that we were trying as hard as we could, so these were quashed every time. You won't be surprised to hear that we didn't buy any more equipment from them ever again.

Back to 2007. Having shed some staff just seven months before in November 2006, we now had to let even more staff go and the company shrank to just ten people. The building was like a ghost ship now, compared with just a few years before when our staff had numbered 23.

I remember a Monty Python skit where a man visits a hotel and rings the door bell, whereupon a doorman comes to greet him. The visitor walks to the main desk and the doorman quickly goes behind the desk, removes his hat and livery jacket and books the visitor in. The same hotel operative rings a loud bell on his desk, after which he speedily dons another hat and coat, runs to the other side of the desk, takes the visitor's luggage and escorts him to his room... You see the picture now! Well, VMI seemed a bit like this at the time.

Back in 2007, without a receptionist, I answered most of the calls myself, and the rental desk consisted of just me and a part-time client contact, but it was mainly me. I answered all calls with gusto, took most of the bookings and negotiating; also did all the invoicing, project-managed all of the important jobs and looked after the marketing, IT, finance and website.

Kevin and a couple of technicians looked after all of the kit prep, return and logistics, and Jay was our solitary driver. The head of accounts had already left when the crisis first broke and this was just as well, since we couldn't have afforded him anyway. By this time however, our accounts assistant, Chau, had really impressed me, and was to become a very important part of VMI's recovery, and today is another of our key Directors.

Some of our larger clients were surprised when the Managing Director kept answering the phone, but I made light of it and explained that I was once again getting 'close to the customer' and enjoyed it, but the truth was that there was no one else.

Mum and Dad still came in to work every day but this didn't last long. It became really awkward continuing to work with Dad, after what had happened in the boardroom.

A week after our fateful meeting, he and I had another argument and after a terse exchange, he looked at me and asked whether I would prefer it, if he were no longer here. I thought about it for a moment and said yes and he left. He wouldn't work at VMI again after this.

The concepts of HD were very technical and this is why my seminars and lectures had been so popular, but now, of course, I had little time for this. Since it was so time-consuming to speak to every client and explain the finer technical considerations of HD which people needed to know, I had the idea to write technical papers and production case studies, and post these onto our internet site. This way, I could point people to our website to educate them, and we would be able to save time on the phone with clients and everybody would be better informed as a result.

These technical pages were very popular – so much so, that I was actually told off by one of my competitors for making this valuable information too accessible to the industry. They argued that this specialist information was their USP (Unique Selling Point) that they traded upon, but my opinion is that 'sharing is caring' and I *wanted* to share this widely and it is something we continue to do today.

Chapter 31. Making it up with Dad

Kevin and I had agreed that we would be paid a low income for a limited time and at least until the worst had passed. During this period, we continued to pay a small income to Mum and Dad.

The company was on its knees and worth very little but I knew that with hard times coming, if I wanted to keep Kevin committed, then I needed to give him something more than just a promise and a low salary. I decided that from now on, we would be paid exactly the same and in time, would also gift him half of my shareholding. Whilst this might sound generous now, my argument was that 50 percent of something, was much better than 100 percent of nothing, and I needed to ensure that he would stay with me through these very testing times, and not be tempted to take a more attractive offer if one should have come along.

That summer was a frenetic blur of energy. We worked very hard to make progress on all fronts whilst also keeping the business going with fewer people than we had thought possible.

Of course, as well as managing the finances of the company, we also needed to buy new equipment as well, since no one wants to hire last year's model of anything. This was hard to achieve, and the finance terms were expensive since we were a shaky company, but it was sadly necessary. Each time that we did this, we would defer some of the VAT to the next quarter to avoid a large unaffordable tax bill, and although making each quarterly VAT return payment was touch-and-go, we always just managed it. I can honestly say that I don't know how we pulled through every time, but I am very happy that we did. Some years later, Nick, my accountant, confided in me that he never actually believed that we would pull through, though happily, he didn't share this with me at the time.

I had a lawyer look at the terms and conditions of the police monitoring contract of our alarm company, to see if there was any scope for us to sue them, but with the absence of any third-party liability, we were more likely to win the lottery. Being a mathematician and understanding the odds, I don't even play the lottery.

The best and most-likely outcome was for us to sue the insurance company but success was no foregone conclusion, since we clearly hadn't fulfilled our obligations as Directors. But if we were successful, then this would give us a slug of money to pay off a large chunk of what we owed our creditors, so this was something which Mum jumped on.

The good news was that an old school friend of mine called Costas was by now a senior solicitor in a firm which specialised in insurance claims. He agreed to take the case and attacked this like a rottweiler. Our insurance company seemed in no hurry to settle, as they kept claiming that there were no grounds for a claim and didn't even really seem to take the threat seriously – "…no police monitoring in place…", they kept saying.

We had several meetings at Costas's very posh offices in London's financial district, and I remember arriving wearing my yellow bike apparel and feeling very out of place on seeing my smartly dressed friend in an elegant suit in the same room together. Eventually though, Costas's perseverance paid off and after a year of action, the insurance company made a settlement offer for £100,000 which we accepted and was really welcome. They called it a 'nuisance' pay-out but I didn't care. Money was money and we didn't have enough of it. We still were obliged to pay the considerable legal costs owed to Costas's firm, though he had agreed that we would pay mates-rates and these were much less than they ought to have been, for which I remain very grateful. Costas ended up making partner and has done extremely well for himself.

Finally, January 2008 arrived and I made it up with Dad. We met for lunch at the 16mm café and I had decided to take a well-earned day off. We sat in the middle of the café and both enjoyed Hennan's terrific quiche, during which someone approached our table to speak with me. Dad dutifully stopped eating and sat back in his seat, expecting me to start engaging with the client - after all, he would have thought, this was business and business comes first. Instead, I told the client that I was busy right now with Dad, and that I would meet with him at his office later that afternoon when I had finished. In doing so, I could see that Dad was impressed and appreciated this gesture, since he too deserved my time.

After lunch, we went downstairs and the two of us watched a private screening of our favourite James Bond film, *Diamonds Are Forever* (of course, what else!).

We were getting on better now, and Dad visited our home in Kent that weekend to celebrate Cheryl's birthday. Just before he left, I asked him if he might like to visit my local village pub with me, as I had never enjoyed sharing a beer with him. He thought about it and declined my offer: "No, not this time but perhaps next time," he said and I think that he really meant this as a genuine offer of friendship to repair our relationship.

Sadly, next time never came and just a week later, whilst on holiday skiing in the Austrian Alps, I received a call from Mum that Dad had suddenly passed away. He had suffered a massive heart attack and had abjectly refused to take the Beta Blocker medication which had been prescribed to him.

For years, the doctors had feared that he had been suffering from an underlying heart condition but he steadfastly refused to believe them or to take their advice. Instead, he firmly believed that as a passionate runner, he wouldn't need to take any medication. "What doesn't kill you, makes you stronger," he would say with a smile. Sadly, he was wrong and paid the ultimate price for this. He was just 67.

We buried him in early March 2008, and I am still sad when I think about the wasted opportunities that we could have had together but console myself that at least I had an opportunity to make things up with him.

Chapter 32. 650,000 Hours

If you love life, don't waste time, for time is what life is made up of. Bruce Lee

At about the turn of the Millennium, I decided to find out how many hours there were in the average life and I was extremely surprised to calculate that 74 years of living equated to just 650,000 hours. What surprised me was that I could actually visualise this number. In fact, until 2006, nobody had ever lived to the required age of 114 years old to survive for a full, one million hours.

Clearly, as a cricketer and one who has never as yet, scored 100 runs, my aim is to make if not a million hours, then at least to survive 100 years.

The thing that surprises me most about life is how much of it, many people seem to spend not actually enjoying it. I, for one, try to enjoy every day and everything that I do, and whilst not everything that I do is enjoyable, at *least* I relish the satisfaction of at least completing a boring task, and then ticking it off on my what-to do list!

I love finding ways to make my life more productive and to find new ways of doing things and making them fun. Don't misunderstand me, they don't always work but I always enjoy the process.

Some years ago, I was given two pairs of cycle socks as a gift, which were made of the best merino wool, and they were really comfortable to wear. Each sock was marked with an L and an R and they fitted my feet perfectly and unusually, there were no flappy bits above the smaller toes which I hate. I looked carefully at how the socks were made, and whilst they were anatomically shaped with the heel sewn at right angles to the ankle, both left and right socks seemed to be made identically, though each fitted only one foot perfectly.

I had a theory that the left sock only became a left sock and similarly with the right sock, as a consequence of me wearing them on one specific foot only. This way, the big toe stretched to take the form of whichever foot I wore it on and this process made them more comfortable to wear.

I tested my theory with a new pair of regular socks and after washing, carefully examined them and did notice that each sock had stretched into a natural left and right sock just through wearing them just once.

Since then, I have been really careful to examine every sock before I put them on, since each has now become either a dedicated left or a right sock and ensure that I continue the process. So, no more flappy bits ! – you try it and you will never look back!

The reason for mentioning this is that even in the mundane, like socks, you can find interest and joy.

The year before Josh was born in 1997, after 26 years of accident-free skiing, I did have an accident and snapped the cruciate ligament of my right knee. This required serious and painful recuperation and two operations, but I worked hard, did all of the exercises required of me and made a perfect recovery. However, in doing so, I needed to devote an entire year to recovery and had to give up sport entirely for this period.

What would I do? I have always felt that every negative situation usually has a silver lining. There is always a good way to consider any situation which develops that might, in some way benefit you. At the very least, it will make you less sad about the situation which does develop but usually I find that I can use it to my advantage.

Today we are in the fifth full week of the 2020 lock down, and I thought that I would use this time to write the book that I have been thinking about since 2011, for example…

Back in 1997, I thought to myself that I had always thought about playing the saxophone and now was my chance.

I visited a music store in London's West End and bought the best saxophone that I could afford, as well as some reeds, a music stand and a book called *How to play Saxophone* and when I returned home, started playing that afternoon. I even took lessons and subsequently played to Josh every day before he was born. When he was a baby, the sound of the saxophone would settle him and even stop him from crying.

When we moved to Kent, I played in my local church accompanying Carol and Claire on keyboard and violin for some years. Then I played for some years accompanying Graham and his group playing music for the local pantomime group called, *Benenden Players*.

We enjoyed playing together so much, that we decided to play our version of extemporised jazz, one evening per week in the loft above Graham's garage and it was a lovely experience. Just like the idiom of the Curate's Egg, some days and some pieces were better than others.

One day, I had one of my 20 original ideas and I suggested that we should host a jazz concert outside on our village green to celebrate the Queen's Diamond Jubilee, in the following summer of 2012. Frankly we weren't good enough to host a jazz concert, and the others should have said 'no' but they didn't. Then time passed, arrangements were made and we continued to practice, and then quite soon it was the day of the concert…

It rained; and we played; and it was OK, and we raised over £1,000 for good causes which was great! The following year, we repeated it again, and it rained again, and our performance was slightly better! I played in the first seven concerts, and the tradition continues today. It all started with a decision that I made about not being able to play sport and then later, having a daft idea.

I like variety. However, whilst I am a competent cricketer who can bowl off-spin and leg spin, which is unusual, I am not the best player in my club. I play saxophone but when I listen to Charlie Parker who was ace, I can't even get close to copying what he played. I love cycling but I can't keep pace with the best in the club that I cycle with.

Over the years I have come to terms with the simple fact, that if you like to try lots of different things, then you must accept that you won't ever be the best at any of them. I am a good husband, father, friend and I do lots of things that I enjoy and I no longer mind anymore not being the best at anything.

The Author playing Tenor Saxophone

Chapter 33. Armed robbery

If you think things can't get worse it's probably only because you lack sufficient imagination. Anon

Be strong because things will get better. It may be storm now but it never rains forever.

Gerard was irritated, as he had been delayed from leaving work and it was now after 7pm. He had an early call-time for tomorrow's BAT commercial shoot and had needed to wait for Jay to return the company's only van to base so that he could take the kit home, because he planned to drive directly to set in the morning.

Jay had already dropped off the van and gone home, and now Gerard was on the camera floor making the final prep to his kit before he left. Despite contravening company policy, he was in the building on his own but he didn't mind. Camera work meant more money for him and with a young family to provide for, this was always welcome.

Suddenly, he heard a crash at the door. "WHAT WAS THAT?," he thought - no one was expected this late. He glanced at the CCTV monitor and could see a blur of activity by the front door and hear lots of noise, so when the intruders burst into the camera room, he wasn't entirely surprised but still felt a sense of shock all the same. This was a ROBBERY!

Three hooded individuals had entered the camera floor wearing balaclavas, and he could see that one of them was carrying a weapon. At first glance, this appeared to be an assault weapon – an

AK47. By the lumbering way that they crashed into the room, they were clearly not professional, and it was obvious from their reaction, that they were as surprised to see him as he had been of them. They had not been expecting the building to be occupied at this time and were evidently stressed.

"WHERE ARE THE F900Rs?" Robber 1 yelled.

Gerard could hear the sound of heavy steps going up the stairs. There were others – maybe three more?

He had to keep his nerve and let his army training take over. He had never thought that the two years National Service for his native South Africa would come in useful, but he also knew that he needed to keep them calm, since these guys were clearly wired.

"WHERE ARE THE F900Rs!" shouted Robber 1 again.

He knew that the Sony F900R camcorder was the most expensive camera on our rental fleet, and also knew that the two that we did own were out on hire. He thought quickly and figured that these guys were not very bright, and they almost certainly wouldn't recognise this specific camera, so he took a calculated risk and showed them another camera with a '900' in its model number. The Panasonic SDX-900 was a much cheaper camera than the Sony, but most importantly, they were also in stock. Robber 1 was clearly the ringleader and he seemed to be OK with the offering, so Gerard breathed easy.

The ringleader continued calling out more demands, "WHERE ARE THE LENSES?"; "WHERE ARE THE HDWS?"...

They were obviously stealing to order and Gerard obliged him as best he could, since he realised that there was no benefit in being beaten up. He was greatly outnumbered by the three hoodlums on the camera floor, and these were just the ones that he could see.

He was surprised though – he might have expected this in South Africa but not in Golders Green!

As he continued to assist the burglars, he was able to take a closer look at the gun that the ringleader was carrying, and could now clearly see that it was actually an air rifle with a Kalashnikov AK47 magazine crudely welded to it, to make it look like a serious weapon. Gerard wasn't fooled and realised that it was just for show but he was not going to be stupid and let the intruders know that he realised this.

A lot of shouting could now be heard coming from upstairs; What were they doing? Suddenly, he heard a loud bang from above his head. The first floor only housed offices, so this must have been the sound of the heavy safe falling to the floor. (It was).

Gerard kicked himself for not thinking of pressing the panic button when he was first alerted to the burglary but now it was too late. They beat and tied him up, confiscated his mobile phone, and then put him in the strong room where the valuable equipment was kept. The robbers had emptied the contents of all of the cases and transported as many of the cameras and lenses that they could carry to the front of the building.

The plan had clearly been for them to escape in the cars that they had arrived in, but now Robber 2 found that he couldn't start the car that he had parked outside and promptly abandoned it, leaving his gloves in the vehicle. The police would later find DNA in the gloves and fingerprints in the car. I told you they weren't smart!

They now changed their plan and decided to steal our van, complete with its company livery, and drove it to the front entrance of the building. More shouting, perspiring, grunting, crashing and banging later, they loaded up and were gone and so was much of our equipment.

Gerard recalls that when being asked later by a police officer if he needed medical attention for the bruise on his face, he declined declaring that 'the robber hit like a girl!' Gerard was never one for losing his cool or catastrophising and as soon as the robbers were out of sight, he wriggled free and discovered that the strong room door wasn't locked. He quickly called the police using the company phone system and then called me. I had just boarded a train to Kent but luckily it was still on the platform at Charing Cross, so I immediately left the station and rode to VMI as quickly as I could.

The *Flying Squad* was London's elite police division who are revered by all of the UK Police Forces and are only ever called out for the most serious crimes. An armed robbery definitely classes as one of these.

They were already at VMI's building when I arrived, and the officers were calm, professional and everyone knew exactly what to do, in stark contrast to the frenzied shouting, crashing and banging of just 30 minutes before.

Since the building was now a crime scene, I sat in the car park, took my laptop out of my rucksack, switched it on and connected to the company WiFi network. I called over a senior officer and showed them a map of London with a flashing red spot at the centre of my screen, and explained to him that this was a live satellite feed, showing the exact location of our company van at this very moment – we could see exactly where the robbers were!

The police told me that they had never before had access to this information so quickly after an incident and were really impressed. Disappointingly though, at the time it was not possible to initiate a chase, but we all watched rivetted nonetheless. When the van stopped for some minutes at a seemingly random location, we correctly ascertained that was the address where the burglars had stopped to unload the loot, and shortly afterwards when the spot stopped, this was the location where our van was eventually abandoned.

It had been a very dramatic day. The police had so much evidence from the burglary and CCTV, that the burglars were eventually caught, convicted and sent to prison for a 12-year term but sadly, in spite of such a hopeful start, we never recovered our equipment.

The good news was that on this occasion, we were to benefit from a nice insurance claim, especially since some of our older equipment would now be replaced with the latest equipment which would help us with our upgrade plan. The bad news was that this would really hurt our already-poor insurance record.

In fact, we had been targeted for robberies so frequently, that this became our fifth robbery and also our fifth insurance claim in two years. We had actually been the victims of a sixth attempt, where intruders had taken out several bricks from our building, before realising that they had broken into a neighbouring unit, so thankfully it never resulted in another burglary or insurance claim. Though to make matters even worse, this last burglary had happened just a week before our annual insurance renewal and understandably, our insurers were no longer keen to reinsure us.

I can't blame them but our premiums more than doubled overnight and we were forced to agree. The insurance company also imposed some new onerous clauses for us, which resulted in us sharing some of the risk with them, so for the next few years, we would only be paid out 50p for every £1 of claim and we had no choice but to accept this.

The armed robbery was a turning point for us, though, as we all decided that we would turn the tables on the burglars – from this time, all of the rental companies would work together.

I called a meeting of all rental company owners and we met one evening in a private room of the *Crown and Two Chairmen* pub in

Dean Street, Soho. We were competitors and had never before worked together or even been in the same room at the same time, so the mood was a bit tense and reminded me of that classic scene of the meeting of the five families in *The Godfather II*!

The mood softened and I explained how we had been targeted for robberies and we all needed to fight back. I played them the CCTV recording of the armed robbery and shared some of the learning points from the training that we had been given to us by *The Flying Squad.*

[If you are interested, they advised us that when confronted with a weapon, to lift our hands up high, surrender and give them whatever they asked for!]

And most importantly, we set up a private network to enable us to collaborate together, when we wanted to share information and this was to work very effectively in the future.

When a year later, we fell victim to a Film School student who went rogue and stole £120K of equipment, and then another, a year later when we were targeted in an elaborate fraud, and lost £300K of kit and which affected multiple rental companies as well, we started to share information about potential and bogus frauds as well. We all collaborate together now and as a consequence, fraud and thefts have largely disappeared from our industry.

This last fraud was really hurtful for me, since the perpetrator used my late Dad to trick me. To explain, Dad had been really popular and hundreds of visitors and well-wishers had attended his funeral. Many though, couldn't attend, so I set up an online memorial to enable those who wanted to, to leave messages of remembrance to share with his family. This confidence trickster had studied this site in detail, and during the nine times that I had met him over an 18-month period (yes nine times even including a business lunch), he regaled stories of Dad working in his Neasden shop. He had never met him at all - it all came from this memorial site. I was fooled and even vouched for him to my competitors who suffered losses as well.

It would *never* happen again and neither would the burglaries. In 2012, we moved VMI to its current building in West London which is in a secure compound complete with 24-hour security.

Since Mum had left VMI shortly after Dad had passed away, Kevin and I now look after insurance and security and we made sure that we learned from every single burglary, theft and fraud. We set up new systems, processes and procedures to ensure that these could not happen again.

The insurance companies worked with us too and trusted us and, true to our word, after 2012 we enjoyed seven claims-free years. High insurance premiums are thankfully no longer a problem for us.

Chapter 34. Early successes...

A wise man will make more opportunities than he finds.   Sir Francis Bacon

Back to 2008 and every small success would see the company becoming just a bit stronger.

At the time, I remember thinking about the metaphor of making a fire in a woodland surrounded by wet wood. Firstly, you have to find some small, dry kindling which isn't easy and then try to light that. Then, once it is glowing, you must very carefully shield it using your hands, since any wind might be enough to put out the glowing embers and our recovery in those days felt just like this. Remaining with my metaphor, the fire wouldn't start to roar allowing it to consume large, thick pieces of damp wood for some years yet but those days would eventually come.

There was to be another sea change of equipment during 2008, which we describe in the TV world, as the Canon 5D Mk II revolution. At the time, camera sensors were really small and they shot pictures with a large depth of field, just like with your mobile phone and they did not look very filmic. But back in 2008, film makers had discovered that the first generation of large-sensor, digital stills cameras (DSLRs) were capable of recording video with a shallow depth of field and this allowed them to shoot low-cost moving images with a 'film look' for the very first time.

Sensing an opportunity, we jumped into this and bought lots of this type of cameras and lenses. Once again, it helped us to carve out another niche for our company, since the equipment was cheap, which was crucial for us at the time, and Kevin could apply his film experience to accessorising it to be acceptable for serious crews. This was very important for professional crews who really didn't want to use it, but were forced to by producers due to its low cost. This successful strategy and the double-digit growth that the company had enjoyed in 2008 and 2009, helped to power us through the recession caused by the financial crisis of 2007/2008.

Then, in September 2009, I visited the annual IBC conference in Amsterdam where, one again, I had another glimpse of the future.

ARRI was the major player in the film world for manufacturing film cameras, lenses and the majority of accessories that film crews love to use, but until 2010, they had only manufactured film cameras which used celluloid film. Not long before this, an organisation called RED had released a digital-film camera which suffered from poor reliability and most professional crews were not fans. However, at the ARRI stand that year, there was a large wooden box containing the electronics of a new prototype camera and next to it, a superb viewfinder. ARRI were playing some incredible images of the Munich Football Stadium at dusk, which were apparently shot with this new ALEV III sensor and these were breathtaking to see.

Kevin was back in London recovering from a recent spinal surgery operation, so I had come alone that year and as soon as I saw it, I knew that we had to buy these cameras, which had been given a code name of Alexa.

VMI wasn't particularly well known to ARRI at the time but I met with a bunch of senior guys and told them that I wanted to buy the first two Alexa cameras *in the world*! It is fair to say that at the time, we didn't have a lot of money but I was certain that we would make them work.

ARRI's executives explained that other than the name, the sensor and the viewfinder, there simply wasn't any more information available, but they planned to release these new cameras in early 2010. Somehow, I persuaded them to agree to sell us the first two Alexa cameras which would be delivered in the UK. I wrote an order onto a piece of paper, took an image of it with my phone and emailed it to ARRI. True to their word, we took delivery of them in early 2010 and the dominance of ARRI in the digital film world had begun.

Until this point, old-school film makers, who are called DPs (Director of Photography) engaged in a long-running debate about whether film or digital was better. Thankfully, although film does continue to be used sometimes today, and is even experiencing a recent revival, this debate has now petered out. However, I understand that the Alexa was so impressive to cinematographers, that ARRI never sold another film camera after its release.

Our goal was to supply equipment for drama productions and by 2011, with the immense popularity of the Alexa and also its extremely limited availability, drama producers were initially biting our hands off to hire them. Here, Kevin came into his own and was able to accessorise our kits exactly to the taste of professional drama crews, to deliver a quality rental service that VMI would become known for in time.

At this time, Ian joined us and we created a new position for him of Head of Drama. Kevin and Ian already knew each other, since Kevin's wife was a focus puller on a drama production for the BBC called *Holby City*, and where Ian also had also worked as DP for many years. Also, Kevin's previous employer used to supply the same production with their kit before he joined VMI.

Compared with me, Ian is very understated about his accomplishments. He was a DP for many years shooting drama and also directed for a time, too. Although he doesn't broadcast this fact, he also is an associate member of the BSC (British Society of Cinematography), which is a really big deal. One day in early 2010, he decided that he had had enough of the early starts and unpredictable schedules, which is the norm for location production, so he decided to hang up his light meter and join VMI. Of course, we were very happy to make a new role for him in the company, and his appointment coincided with the arrival of our first two ARRI Alexa cameras, so he started work in earnest.

Drama is a really tough market to break into. Drama crews tend to work together and go from one production to the next and mostly stay in their genre, not tending to veer into feature or commercials work. Drama line producers, who make the final decision about where to hire their cameras from, do the same. They hire the equipment from a very small pool of companies and back in 2011, this absolutely did not include us.

Kevin, Ian and I were a really good fit and worked together well. Kevin would present the kit the way that the drama crews expected, Ian would already know the crews and line producers and I was good at raising the finance and making the numbers work. Initially, with only two Alexa cameras, we were able to supply equipment for just one show at a time and *Friday Night Dinner* was one of our earliest productions.

VMI's Golders Green building was woefully inadequate for us by this stage, as the low ceilings were claustrophobic, the camera test rooms were up some narrow stairs, and equipment is large and heavy, parking was very restrictive too and storage and prep space was so limited, that all of the available floor area would be taken up with just one major job.

As 2011 drew to a close, I was working on my next business plan.

We needed to move to a more secure location and had our sights on a brand-new building in Acton to move to. However, to be able to afford the massive increase in costs, we would need a sizeable increase in revenue and profit.

In mid-2010, I wrote a 'bet-the-company' business plan, which would see us buying sufficient equipment to supply five concurrent drama projects, and then we would be able to afford to move into this new building.

§

Chapter 35. Remote teams.

It seemed the world was divided into good and bad people. The good ones slept better... while the bad ones seemed to enjoy the waking hours much more.   Woody Allen

Getting the best out of people is a real art and without a great role model or mentor at the start of my career, I made a lot of mistakes before I was able to master the delicate art of management.

We are all totally unique – one-offs, built to order by our parents, so it entirely stands to reason that managing people doesn't work with a 'one-size, fits all' approach.

The paper tower exercise of my formative MBA years showed me how teams might suffer if too many people wanted to take charge, but what I would subsequently learn was that even the way that people process and share their ideas, could influence a team's harmony.

Every day I generate lots of ideas and I know that many of them are poor, but when I am with like-minded people, I can fire new ideas at them and by bouncing these between us, they can evolve and improve. I would describe my idea of brainstorming to be like passing a rough slab of wet clay to a colleague, who after scrutinising it, cuts half of it away with a large knife before adding another slab of clay to roughly change its shape, after which they pass it back to me. This process can go on for some time and each time, progressively finer changes are applied until eventually, we have a finished plan that we both agree on, and which has totally improved my original idea.

Dad didn't work this way, though I didn't realise this for many, many years. He would do all of the crafting in his head by working and refining his ideas over several days without mentioning them to anyone. Finally, when he felt that his idea was ready for sharing, he would present me with the equivalent of a finely finished sculpture that he had even burnished. No wonder that he didn't act kindly when I took my large machete to it before adding another slab of wet clay onto one side before passing it back to him as a suggestion of how I felt his design might actually be improved!

Dad and really didn't work together well but at the time, I had no conception why and I wish I could have learned this lesson earlier. Being aware of how you and others think and work is crucial if you want to work effectively together and enjoy the process.

During my time, I have learned that everyone has their own way of working and is motivated differently. In my role as the company 'conductor', it is my job to try to learn the individual traits of each person, and thus allow everyone to be able to work in their own way and thrive.

The wonderful 2002 film, *My Big Fat Greek Wedding* has a scene where the wife explains to her daughter that in Greek culture, whilst the man may be the head of the household, the woman is the neck, who moves the head and can influence where the man looks! I am not sure about the legitimacy of the man/woman differential here, but my job can sometimes be a bit like being the neck and helping my teams to see a different perspective that they might not have considered before.

One day I met a driver from another company who was waiting for his hire to be ready. I asked him who he was and he told me that he was 'just the driver'. I told him that, at this specific moment he was the most important person from his organisation and he was really surprised to hear this. I told him that the bosses and client contacts of his company didn't often meet the clients – only the drivers did. If he was rude, then this would reflect badly on his company but if he was happy, helpful and represented them well, then they might have a better impression of his firm.

I explained further that if the client was worth perhaps, £50,000 per year and they recommended his firm to five others, then we could imagine that he was perhaps worth £250,000. Assuming that they continued trading with his company for some more years, then he alone would be looking after a potential million-pound client right now! He told me that he had never considered this before. Everyone needs to feel that they play a valuable role in their organisations and I have never forgotten this important lesson.

Working from home, I had to invent new ways to motivate and manage remote teams and I adopted my usual approach of trial and error, seeing what worked and then refining it until it worked perfectly.

I originally thought that it might be possible to write up a script for the client contacts which worked for me and train others on how to use it, just like Jordan Belfort did in the 2013 film, *The Wolf of Wall Street* but found that this approach didn't work for us. I learned that it was much better to train people on how to use the business tools available and then, let them to put their own stamp on it and in doing so, they would also have some ownership of it too.

In time I was able to find ways to keep people engaged and motivated, without being at work every day but it was still important for me to have some face to face time with both my teams, clients and suppliers, so I reserved Tuesdays for this.

When my clients would ask me to meet them for a meeting, say on Wednesday, I would thank them and suggest that Tuesday was better for me and nine times out of ten, they agreed. In this way, I manage to squeeze all of my meetings into one day per week.

Also very important for me was when I visited the company each week, I made sure that I made time to speak with everyone who was working there on that day. With more staff and two sites today, this is harder to achieve but I still try to adopt this approach and it has worked well for me.

Chapter 36. Bet-the-company

Take care to get what you like or you will be forced to like what you get. George Bernard Shaw

It is surprising that the computing giant IBM, was initially a me-too typewriter manufacturer back in the late 1950s. Their bet-the-company moment came in 1964 when they released their first computer and made the transition to becoming a computer manufacturer.

So too did Richard Branson in 1984, when he launched Virgin Atlantic with a vision to make air travel exciting again, and turn his company into an airline, from previously selling music.

Most companies have a bet-the-company moment at some point in their history and for VMI, this was to come in 2012, when we decided to become a drama camera rental house.

We had decided to increase our drama fleet by making a huge investment in equipment to enable us to equip five concurrent double-camera drama kits. If we achieved this, then the additional revenue generated would enable us to afford both the repayments on the new equipment and also the rent on a new warehouse.

This plan wouldn't work without a new building since our current building was already too small for us, and we couldn't afford the rent on a larger warehouse without the additional business. This was a brave decision to make at the time.

We'd had one misstep already, back in October 2008, when our poor burglary record forced us to look for a secure location to move to, and we had initially decided on Pinewood Studios, but after more than a year of negotiations and planning, this fell through and we were to remain in Golders Green for four more years, spending money instead on improving both our existing facility and better security.

By late 2011 and after four concurrent years of almost 15 percent business annual growth, we were bursting at the seams in our present building. We had operated from here for more than twenty years and couldn't put the inevitable move off any longer.

Continuing to operate from our current location, aside from it being quite unpleasant for the staff, was actually bad for business, since we were continually forced to shuffle equipment around from one place to another, just so that we could free space to operate and this was highly inefficient.

In fact, lack of space caused us to make several errors too, since equipment was frequently misplaced, and occasionally boxes were missed when loading vans, which made us look incompetent and necessitated repeat deliveries. Vans had to be loaded and unloaded wherever they could park in our small, dog-leg car park and every heavy flight case had to be carried in and out of the building by hand, sometimes for a fair distance.

The rapid take-up of the ARRI Alexa cameras gave me great confidence that we could compete in the drama camera market, but our existing chaotic building did not give clients an appropriate impression of our business, and both Kevin and Ian were reluctant to invite crews to visit our warehouse. The camera test rooms were the wrong size and equipment had to be carried upstairs in order to test and then downstairs again, to load the vans. We didn't even have a dedicated lens projection room which was expected from a serious supplier, so winning any drama production would be a triumph against the odds.

Until this time, we had only supplied a few dramas with equipment and none of these were well known. When drama line producers asked what productions we had previously equipment for, we would answer *Friday Night Dinner, Sensitive Skin and Blue-Orange* but they wouldn't have heard of any of them. They would ask whether we had supplied any others and we would pause before answering quietly, "no."

If we were to be successful, then we needed to win a flagship drama that everyone had heard of; we would also need a larger drama fleet with a good choice of lenses and an impressive building. We needed to achieve all of these now, else it would fail. No pressure then!

Each drama kit used about half a million pounds worth of equipment, so if we wanted to supply five concurrent dramas, then we would need to spend about £2m now, and this would need to include several sets of expensive film prime lenses too, to bolster our limited inventory.

This was a lot more equipment than we had ever purchased in one go before, and I was aware of the risks but needed to quantify them to justify this decision. So I wrote a fully costed business plan and performed a comprehensive sensitivity analysis to show what might happen if we didn't deliver - obviously, certain business failure. At the same time, we also found a suitable building in Acton which could accommodate our business growth for the next 10 years or so, and negotiated a ten-year lease with an easy start for our first 12 months, after which we would pay full-whack. We also commissioned a design and build company for the fit-out which was to cost an absolute fortune but the good news was that we had a freehold building to sell which would pay for it.

We saved money wherever we could, including me selling our old building and saving £15K in fees. This is a little less impressive than it sounds, since the buyer was actually the owner of the business operating next door to us, but I was able to negotiate a higher price than the professional agents thought possible.

We had our sights firmly on winning the ITV Drama flagship series of Agatha Christie's *Poirot* and *Marple* and also *Mr Selfridge*, and all three productions would be shooting during 2012. Our strategy was that, if we could win and deliver-on these quality dramas, then no one would ever doubt our credentials again and our drama reputation would be secure.

We pushed as hard as we could to win them and with Ian and Kevin's help, managed to persuade ITV to give us a chance with *Poirot* and *Marple*. It really helped that Ian was friends with the line producer of both series, and I remember that he was concerned about whether we could really deliver. He asked Ian straight, could we *really* deliver, since it was *his* reputation on the line? Ian promised him sincerely that we could and the deal was done – we were now supplying cameras for *Poirot* and *Marple*. We did a really good job too and the line producer and crew were so impressed with our services that we would continue to work with them all on many projects in the future.

It was a close contest with *Mr Selfridge* and we made the final shortlist of two companies but lost out to a worthy competitor. Luckily, several other projects took their place including *Threesome*, *Some Girls* and then later, *Midsomer Murders* and more but it was crucial that we had bagged *Poirot*. Once we told line producers that we had supplied the cameras for *Poirot* and *Marple*, then no further explanation was necessary and we transitioned to becoming a potential camera supplier for all future UK TV dramas.

By the end of 2012, we had successfully delivered on five concurrent dramas for most of the year, and I had hit all of my targets. Of course, this meant that we could afford the rent on our new building too. The business continued to enjoy double digit growth for much of the rest of the decade. More quality productions and happy crews followed and over time, our reputation soared.

Dad always claimed to me that we should aim for profit first, but I disagree, as my experience has been that, as a rental company, we should primarily aim for customer service, after which both revenue and profit follows.

We completed the fit-out of the Acton building in time to move the entire company in January 2012. When it was finished, it looked really professional and gave just the impression that we wanted to convey to clients and crews. It was also a much nicer place to work with lots of daylight and huge amounts of space which none of us were used to. Acton contained a dedicated lens projection room, two test rooms and a garage, complete with air lock and electric shutter, so that at last we could load and unload with complete security. Also for the first time, we were able to use pallet trucks to allow large consignments of equipment to be moved around the building with ease.

I was very keen that this building would be as energy-efficient as possible, so we imported £10,000 of LED light fittings directly from China, since in 2012 these weren't widely available in the UK. We also converted our existing large sodium downlighters to LED which used just 10 percent of the power but were just as bright. We fitted plastic floor tiles, which had been manufactured from recycled Tetrapaks which kept the place warm, and even had one made with our logo printed onto it, which looked really smart at our main entrance. Large pictures of our equipment and past productions were hung to convey how great our gear was, and the place looked white, clean and tidy. Everything was designed with elegance and efficiency in mind, and DPs still describe our building as being like a Formula-1 workshop - something we always like to hear.

As the business grew, so did the staff and, over time, new divisions were added to the business. In 2015, we opened a Bristol branch which specialised in supplying Natural History productions and stocked some very long lenses and specialist grip equipment like a stabilised camera mount which can fix to boats or off-road vehicles.

In 2017, we opened the VMEDIA division, which was a specialist rental facility for supplying large, fast memory cards for 4K productions and which are surprisingly expensive to buy. Then, later in 2018, we added power to its product range too. VMEDIA today, supplies international features and dramas productions for the popular Video-on-Demand channels which have an insatiable appetite for making new productions.

The company grew and so did the people. Remember the lowly Accounts Assistant back in 2007, who was pulling his hair out to pay the bills when we had no cash? Well, Chau was made Financial Director back in 2017, and Ian became Commercial Director at the same time and Stuart, our Rental Desk Manager, became our fifth Director recently in December 2019.

Whilst we are now a sizable rental company with a wide rental fleet, it has not all be plain sailing, with challenges presented by shocks to the economy caused by snap elections and the uncertainty caused by the Brexit referendum. Even now, as I write these pages, the COVID-19 crisis has stopped the entire worldwide production industry for working for some months.

However, having a strong team of professional, competent people who really care about the business means that whatever challenges are thrown at us, we can now handle it. There really is safety in numbers.

Chapter 37. MAG

A goal is not always meant to be reached; it often serves simply as something to aim at. Bruce Lee

Shortly after moving to Kent, I started an annual tradition in our house which we have maintained and look forward to at the end of every Christmas break. New Year's Eve which for many is a raucous occasion, instead for us is a quiet family evening at home, enjoying a cold spread of our favourite foods, followed by an event which we call, *The Book*.

After we have enjoyed eating dinner together, we all retire to the living room, dim the lights, play soft music and bring out our special book which only comes out once per year on this specific evening. I open a fresh page and we discuss the year which has passed and I write a summary of the main events which we agree have shaped this current passing year. As I flick back a few pages, I turn to Cheryl's page which lists the New Year's resolutions which she had committed to for this year and had written exactly one year ago at this very same event. As a family, we discuss each aim in turn and Cheryl gives an honest appraisal of whether she had been successful in achieving it and if so, receives a tick.

After completing her last years' resolutions, we turn to a fresh page. And here, Cheryl writes a new list of resolutions that she wishes to achieve in the coming year and usually adds the ones that she didn't complete this year. Everyone take part and if friends are visiting, they add their pages too.

We really look forward to this occasion and it helps us all to reflect on the year gone by and also look forward to the year ahead. We always insist that *The Book* is not competitive, but I confess I do love to tick off as many of my resolutions as possible!

I always add an entry to my list to tick off one item from my bucket list, which is a list of all of the events which I would like to achieve before I 'kick the bucket.' As you might expect, this is quite an eclectic selection, which includes skiing on all seven continents of the world, performing a ski jump, scoring a century at cricket and free-diving without pressurised air to catch a sea bass with a harpoon followed by cooking and eating it. Over the past few years, I have rarely been successful in achieving a tick against this specific entry though! However, I am happy to report that this year, I will receive a tick for writing my book, which has been on my list since 2011.

On 31 December 2016, I had a crazy idea and announced to my family that I wanted to raise £10,000 for MAG that year...

Some background here is required: About five years before, I had read a book called *One Step Beyond* by an author called Chris Moon which opened my eyes to the horror of landmines. The book was an autobiography of a marathon runner who had had an interesting life before being blown up by a land mine and in which he had lost both an arm and a leg. After he recovered, Moon continued to run marathons including the fabled *Marathon des Sables* which crosses the Sahara Desert and is accurately described as the toughest footrace on earth.

I was really inspired by both his story, grit and determination but also moved by the inequity of the tragedy that landmines have on so many children, who are entirely innocent of the conflicts which they are involved in. I was also impressed with the bravery of those who work to clear them. After reading this book, I decided to collect for a mine clearing organisation called MAG who work tirelessly all around the world to help the 60 million or so people who live in conflict zones and in fear of landmines every day. MAG have made a commitment to help to make the world landmine free by 2020, which I feel is really important, since every day around 20 people somewhere in the world are blown up and half of them are children.

I had been collecting for MAG since 2010 and some of the profits from every jazz concert that we had ever held were donated to them, but this was just one of several good causes that we donated to, so my share never amounted to more than a couple of hundred pounds and I felt that I could do more.

I had made this announcement to my family without any forethought and when Cheryl asked me how I was going to raise this impressive sum of money, I told her quite truthfully that I had no idea. However, I wrote an entry on my New Year's resolution page of *The Book* and the ideas soon started coming.

A month later, I launched the *Superheroes Campaign*. I think that this name actually came from Gary, who now ran our Bristol division and it made me laugh, so the name stuck. My idea was that like *The Fireflies*, 11 years before, a group of cyclists would ride on an impressive journey and we would ask companies to donate money with sponsorship, which hopefully should raise £10,000.

For an impressive journey, it made sense to ride bicycles from London to Amsterdam and to schedule this for September of that year, since we would be visiting the annual international IBC conference in Amsterdam anyway. I thought that a challenge to ride there would help to encourage the major manufacturers, distributers and dealers to support us who would be taking part at the same event and whom we could meet there to congratulate us.

Another consideration was that since lot of riders had expressed an interest in taking part but couldn't make the IBC dates (nor cost), I decided to arrange a second ride from London to Bristol which we had planned for the summer and would enable more cyclists to take part and thus help with fundraising.

Arranging the first year was really tough, since everything was new. I arranged the rides, the routes, the health and safety, the places to stop, the sponsors, the jerseys, hotels etc etc. Above all, it was tough to persuade so many corporate sponsors to part with their money but eventually, I had confirmed 35 of them and we managed to raise £12,500 which was fantastic. The 150-mile ride from London to Amsterdam was in its infancy and our first year included just two riders, myself and a DP called Jay, who had pestered me for years to ride with him to Amsterdam.

Encouraged by our first year's success, we repeated this for a second year and managed to secure 62 sponsors and raise £22,500, which was really impressive. We increased our numbers to five riding from London to Amsterdam that year, though one rider's wife fell sick the day before we were due to leave and he missed the ride, so only four of us ended-up riding together.

At one of the many parties that I attended at IBC that year, my friend Yevgeny whispered to me that he would like to ride with us next year. Yev is a larger-than life character, who has a reputation for hard drinking and hard partying. He is generally the last to leave at all of the big industry parties but at this time did NOT have a reputation for either healthy-living or exercise, so I was surprised by his offer.

"Yev, London to Amsterdam is a long ride," I stated. "We ride for 100 miles on the first day and this is not for the faint hearted," but he was not dissuaded.

"Barry," he barked in his thick Russian accent, "I *will* ride next year with you, but please – keep it secret!" The look of utter determination in his eyes seemed to convey seriousness but I wasn't altogether convinced.

He then whispered to everyone in the room who would listen, that he would be a Superheroes rider the following year and ride from London to Amsterdam on a bicycle but they too were sworn to secrecy!

His co-director, Jon, was very amused and approached me with an offer that I could not refuse.

"Barry, CVP will sponsor the Superheroes with £2,000 on two conditions," he said. "Firstly, I won't do the ride and secondly, you must *not* let Yev off the hook!"

Of course I agreed to this, as £2,000 was way more than the £200 that I had asked most companies to sponsor. Every month I would ring up Yev and ask him if he had bought a road bike yet – and he would tel me "no, not yet." But eventually in in April of the following year, he told me that he had finally bought a bike. Then two-months later in June, he confessed that he had actually started riding it.

We were scheduled to cycle to Amsterdam in just 10-weeks time.

I wanted to go out on a high in our third and final year, so I pushed really hard for sponsors, and between us all, we managed to secure 92 corporate sponsors and raised a record £27,500 for MAG.

Finally, the day of the ride arrived and the eight riders met at VMI in time to make a prompt 8am start, all wearing their smart Superhero jerseys which had been designed and printed to include 93 sponsor logos on every spare bit of material. Chau and my son, Josh were our support team and would feed and water us on our way to Amsterdam, driving a company van. It was the first time that Josh had driven on the continent too and he did really well. His reward was that I had promised him a hero's evening of celebrations in Amsterdam!

Chau and Jay had supported us on almost every previous ride, so it was fitting that at least one of them was with us on our last trip.

Sadly, Jay was too sick to make this last event, although he helped us from home by making regular social networking posts to keep our sponsors and supporters engaged.

The first day started very well to beautiful sunshine and everyone was in high spirits. I carried a powerful portable speaker on my bike pumping out the Superhero playlist that Josh and I had prepared, which was a mashup of jazz-funk, R&B, RAP, 60s Do-Wop, jazz and some 80s sing-along hits but pretty much all of the tracks had a strong beat in common to keep us going.

When we reached the half way mark of 80km (50 miles), I complemented Yev on having ridden further than he had ever ridden before.

I shall never forget his response, which came with his typically thick Russian accent with a slightly angry tone.

"Barry, my ARSE is on FIRE! How far do we have to go?"

We laughed out loud and told him that this was the highest point on the route (not true); that it was all downhill from here (also not true) and that from here it wasn't really that far either (err…).

Suffice to say, we all arrived at Harwich that evening in time for the sleeper ferry that would take us to Holland and all were still in one piece. Then after a restful sleep, we left the Hook of Holland by bike in the driving rain for the third year in a row. To this day, I have never ridden a bicycle in Holland when it hasn't rained but I think that this is just bad luck!

We did go out that evening to celebrate having raised over £60,000 during the three years of the Superheroes rides but sadly, Josh had fallen ill and had to go back to the hotel early, so missed out on his epic night of partying that had long been planned.

All of these memories and all of the money raised for this good cause came from a crazy idea and not being prepared to give up.

I continue to support the MAG charity today, which in 2019 alone, helped one million people to live free from fear and you too are also helping them, since 10 percent of all of the net proceeds from this book are being donated to MAG, so thank you too!

www.maginternational.org

§

Chapter 38. Happiness

Happiness is nothing more than good health and a bad memory. Albert Schweitzer

The happiness of your life depends upon the quality of your thoughts. Marcus Aurelius

I used to be very impatient and wanted to be the best at everything. Now I find comfort being in my own skin and not being in such a hurry all of the time.

I used to consider arriving early for any event to be a waste of my time which I hated. This would include waiting for trains, so I would cut my journey time so finely, that I was always stressed before I left, stressed on the journey too and we would sometimes be late, which would really irritate Cheryl.

I have since broken this bad habit and leave now 10 minutes earlier than I used to and always know that I have time to spare. As a result, I am calmer *and* always arrive on time. I can attest that some life lessons can be this simple but we have to come the conclusion ourselves and then *decide* to break this cycle in order to change and enjoy life more.

I have met some incredible people on my journey and in some small way, their influence has moulded me to be the person that I have become, just as I have changed them too.

Jay started with the company in 2005 and has been there ever since I can remember. He is such a lovely guy, never has a bad thing to say about anyone and is a true inspiration to all who have ever the pleasure of meeting him.

Jay Patel, 2019

From his daily uplifting posts which he shares on social media, you would have no idea that he is fighting cancer for the second time in his life. He continues to do this with the single aim of wanting to share and make others happy.

It was one of Jay's postings in the past that inspired me with the idea of making *The Happiness Book.* This is a book which lives on my mantlepiece and every page contains a written memory of a great day that I have experienced. Its first entry was my birthday last year, when my family made a big fuss of me, Josh prepared a lovely family meal, we watched a film, went for a lovely walk… Every time I flick through the book, I remember happy days and it makes me smile. I heartily recommend that everyone make their own Happiness Book.

Running the company used to consume every available moment of my life and honestly, some of those times were not pleasant. Now though, with a better team, stronger balance sheet, good financial controls, tight quality standards and money in the bank, running the company is now so much easier, and more fun than it used to be.

I can't say that it has been an easy voyage, and I have faced a lot of challenges along the way, but I am reminded of an ancient Japanese proverb which states that, *the only way to enjoy a delicious meal is to have endured hunger.* Using this same metaphor, I have endured a lot of hunger.

However, for the first time in my life, I find myself with more time to allow me to concentrate on other strategies, and also more time to think. Over this last year, I have been working to design and launch a new apprenticeship standard, which I hope will provide young people with a structured way to enter our industry. This is as an alternative to avoid the huge expense and uncertainty of attending university, and which isn't necessarily so useful in our creative sector.

Our syndicate of rental companies now works together to share good practice, with a common aim of all reducing our carbon footprints too, and helping to make our businesses more sustainable.

In our company, Chau started a group which he calls *The Lunch Club,* where people cook for each other during the lunch breaks. He and I have also become accomplished bakers, and we enjoy competitive sourdough baking and bringing our cakes and bread into the office for others to enjoy and tell us which they prefer!

Most of all, my friends and family are very important to me. In Kent last year, we started the *Phileas Fogg Society* inspired by the Jules Verne classic novel *Around the World in 80 days*. The idea was that friends would meet every two weeks to enjoy a gastronomic tour of the world. We take it in turns to visit each other's houses and cook meals using recipes of countries of our choosing, in order to pretend that we are engaging in a virtual world tour!

I love to cook and to do this with the excuse of sharing our creations with friends of the *Phileas Fogg Society,* just makes it a bit more of an experience, which is what I like to do.

My life has had lots of twists, turns and drama, and my wife Cheryl has been with me throughout the entire journey. I can honestly say that I could not have done this without her. She has been my rock and whilst I am very much an advocate for equality, it always helps to have a supportive partner who can prepare a home-cooked meal and provide a sympathetic ear if things aren't going well. She knows me well enough not to dismiss my 'Hair Brained Schemes' without hearing my reasoning first – *raising £10,000 for MAG…*

I receive a lot of Facebook notifications from past employees who are now doing interesting things around the world. Dado, who was our first and only AVID Wizard, now lives in LA with his wife and is another of those people, who on meeting him, leaves a lasting impression. He runs an organisation called *Colorspace* and at one presentation that we gave together in London a few years ago, made the announcement that he considered me to be the only boss who could ever manage him. Knowing him as well as I do now, I think that this is quite plausible!

Another former work colleague lives in Zimbabwe and he recently shot a feature film which recently won an international film award.

We had lunch together last year when he was in London and regaled his fond memories of his time at Golders Green when he started his career as a technician.

Several other past employees are now camera assistants and camera operators, who shoot features and dramas and they all have their story to tell. When I see them, they share with me how much fun they had during their time with the company. I feel privileged to have been part of their journey.

Working with Mum and Dad was never easy and certainly nothing that I had ever planned to do, however, my experiences have made me the person who I am today. I remember at the time thinking how brave Dad was in his early twenties to have started a company the way that he did. However difficult my journey was, I do owe my parents a debt of gratitude for the opportunity that working for them has afforded me.

Whilst I am now an entrepreneur, just like Bilbo Baggins of Tolkein's *The Hobbit*, who himself became an accidental hero, I don't mind admitting that my journey was also largely by chance, rather than by design. It is easy now to consider where I might have been had I made different choices but that isn't very helpful because I didn't make those choices. I didn't choose to become a mathematics professor or a derivatives dealer in New York. Instead, I stayed in London and looked after my parents.

I like to ponder the concept that we are the sum product of all of our choices, and I like where I have finally ended up.

Ultimately, Dad was correct when he stated that "you get what you aim for."

My advice is to be true to your values and treat others the way that you yourself would want to be treated. Use your time wisely. Enjoy life. Be kind and look after your family.

If you do this, then like me, hopefully you will enjoy your life to the full.

I sincerely hope that you have enjoyed this book and would REALLY appreciate if you could leave a review for me, which will help me to spread my happiness message.

Thank you – now have a great life.

§

www.fullexperienceliving.com

The Pigeon Steps school of motivation
The best way to complete a difficult task… is to begin. Barry Bassett

I wrote this to be a chapter in the book but it didn't really fit and since so many of us find self-motivation difficulty, I have kept this at the end just in case you find it helpful.

If you think about starting any big task, then it is easy to be daunted by the sheer scale of the challenge and to let this dissuade you from actually making a start.

I think that we are all guilty of making this error but I find that simply *deciding* to start, is a great way to begin, and starting was what my Dad found very hard to do, and which was why he would often look at the word *GODO* written upon the paper in his workshop and also the reason that it became part of our family vocabulary.

This book is an example of my own procrastination, since I first had the idea of writing an account of my recovery from near-certain bankruptcy back in 2011, and wrote an outline plan but never went any further than this. I ALWAYS had other things to do, however, it remained on the back of my mind (and appeared on my New Year's resolutions for 8 straight years with a cross) until a Government-imposed lock-down in 2020, which gave me 12 straight weeks of not doing my regular job. Then on the eighth day of the lock-down, I decided to begin, so I sat down and started and this book is the result. This is GODO at work!

My approach has three simple parts to it and each are crucial:

1. Break down the huge task into lots of little tasks which are actually quite manageable.
2. Begin
3. Promise yourself a treat when you complete each mini task

I have adopted this approach my entire life, and it has enabled me to complete some really big projects whilst remaining entirely in control and keeping my sanity! I will even go so far as to say that I have usually enjoyed the projects too!

So, to begin a really huge task, what do you need to do is to sit down with a good cup of coffee and a blank sheet of paper (or computer with a word processor) and start to write a list of all of the large tasks in order to complete this project.

Example Plan: Build a Bridge
Major Tasks: Design the Bridge; Buy the Materials; Choose a Building Company; Build the Bridge…

Then break each of the large tasks into smaller tasks and those into yet smaller tasks.

Minor Tasks: Look at existing bridge designs; Choose preferred style; Find an architect who works in this style;…

OK, now you have a plan.

Now you have to decide to start. Again, this is more easily said, than done but and this is the MOST important factor to gauge whether you will be successful or not. Your first task has to be both small, easy and also possible to complete.

So looking at your **First Minor Task** of *Look at existing bridge designs* - recognise that this is EASY enough to not put you off starting!

Having written it down, you need to start and complete the very first minor task and then you can tick it off on your schedule.

Lastly, it is crucial to find ways to reward yourself to keep you motivated, and then look forward to completing your first small mini-task.

In 2007 when I cycled from Geneva to Cannes through the Alps, we would climb each mountain for several hours and for much of the climbs we were below the tree-line and you could not see much beyond 100m in front of you, so it was really hard to see any progress at all.

We would cycle uphill for hours and I knew that it would be hard to keep myself motivated, so my strategy was to bring along a compact altimeter with me and monitor my altitude as I cycled. My mini goal became climbing just 50m of altitude. 50m is easy but climbing of 2,000m is hard. The full ascent would see me achieving 40 of these mini goals, so each time I climbed 50m, I would feel great and THAT was my reward and of course, eventually arriving at the summit was even better!

Perhaps your reward might be to watch NETFLIX after completing your assignment or chapter, or perhaps to enjoy a biscuit or perhaps even just to tick-off an item on you what-do-do list, which is often my motivation, but whatever it is, enjoy the satisfaction of starting and then make sure that you enjoy the reward for completing your task too.

A final tip which I still find useful and do today. When I was studying, as soon as I had completed a study session, I would intentionally leave my books open and set up, ready for the next time that I would start studying. It was really important that the book was open at the appropriate page with a blank sheet of paper and pen at the ready, so when I sat down, I wouldn't have to think about what I needed to do. If you do this, then you can't talk ourselves out of starting, since by now, you have already begun...!. I even used this approach when writing this book, albeit computer left on, word processor document open at the right place...

Chapter over and book complete, I am ready for my reward now. A shower and a lovely cup of coffee!

My son Josh did a great job of illustrating this book but I wanted to share some of the history of the company and especially include a few videos, including the one of the wacky-custard sports day, which obviously isn't possible in a paperback or eBook.

So if you are interested, then do visit my website, which I setup specifically to accompany the book.

I have uploaded full colour images, my favourite recipes and a positivity community on my website:

www.fullexperienceliving.com

Sincere thanks to all of my friends who proofread my book on WhatsApp and to whom I shared my early ideas with. Also, to Adrian Pennington for proofreading the book and for making 2,800 suggestions on what I had considered was a completed draft!

To Cheryl and Josh, for patiently listening to my chapters every day as I wrote them and also a special thanks to Josh for his amazing cover design and illustrations

.

We are the sum product of all of our life's choices. Wayne Dwyer

§

Printed in Great Britain
by Amazon

56059563R00125